THE BIOPSYCHOLOGY COLOURING BOOK

THE
BIOPSYCHOLOGY
COLOURING
BOOK

**SUZANNE HIGGS
ALISON COOPER
JONATHAN LEE**

Los Angeles I London I New Delhi
Singapore I Washington DC I Melbourne

Los Angeles | London | New Delhi
Singapore | Washington DC | Melbourne

SAGE Publications Ltd
1 Oliver's Yard
55 City Road
London EC1Y 1SP

SAGE Publications Inc.
2455 Teller Road
Thousand Oaks, California 91320

SAGE Publications India Pvt Ltd
B 1/I 1 Mohan Cooperative Industrial Area
Mathura Road
New Delhi 110 044

SAGE Publications Asia-Pacific Pte Ltd
3 Church Street
#10-04 Samsung Hub
Singapore 049483

Editor: Donna Goddard
Editorial assistant: Esme Carter
Production editor: Ian Antcliff
Copyeditor: Jo North
Proofreader: Emily Ayers
Marketing manager: Camille Richmond
Cover design: Shaun Mercier
Typeset by: C&M Digitals (P) Ltd, Chennai, India

Library of Congress Control Number: Available

British Library Cataloguing in Publication data

A catalogue record for this book is available from the British Library

ISBN 978-1-5297-3091-3 (pbk)

CONTENTS

Why choose a colouring book for learning Biological Psychology? ix
About the authors xi

1 Structure of the nervous system 1

1.1 The peripheral and central nervous system 2
1.2 Anatomical directions 3
1.3 Terms used to indicate direction and orientation in the nervous system 4
1.4 Key features of the human brain 5
1.5 The lobes of the brain 6
1.6 The brainstem 7
1.7 Slice of the spinal cord with spinal nerves 8
1.8 The ventricles of the brain 9

2 Communication in the nervous system 11

2.1 Traditional representation of a neuron 12
2.2 Oligodendrocytes (glial cells) 13
2.3 Cross section of the cell membrane of a neuron 14
2.4 A representation of the neuronal cell membrane with a K+ channel and the Na+K+–ATPase 15
2.5 The action potential 16
2.6 The synapse between a presynaptic neuron and postsynaptic neuron 17
2.7 The key structures of the synapse 18
2.8 Exocytosis 19
2.9 Postsynaptic transmission 20
2.10 The tripartite synapse 21
2.11 Neurotransmitters 22

3 Drugs and the nervous system: psychopharmacology 23

3.1 Time course of action of drugs according to route of administration 24
3.2 Dose response curve illustrating action of an agonist, antagonist and inverse agonist 25
3.3 The therapeutic index 26
3.4 Change in dose response curve with tolerance and sensitisation 27
3.5 Dose response effects for alcohol 28
3.6 Ionotropic and metabotropic receptors 29
3.7 The GABA-A receptor complex 30
3.8 Effects of cocaine on dopamine neurotransmission 31
3.9 Effects of morphine on opioid neurotransmission 32
3.10 The action of nicotine in the brain 33
3.11 Caffeine binding to adenosine receptors 34

4 Development and degeneration in the nervous system 35

4.1 The structure of DNA 36
4.2 Meiosis and mitosis 37
4.3 Neurulation 39
4.4 The brain develops from a tubular structure 40

4.5   Migration of neurons during formation of the foetal brain   42
4.6   A neuron migrates along glial scaffolding   43
4.7   Axon guidance   44
4.8   Apoptosis   45
4.9   Neuropathology of Parkinson's disease   46
4.10 Brain with Huntington's disease   47
4.11 Treatment for Parkinson's disease: L-DOPA   48
4.12 Genes with neurotransmission related functions impacted in schizophrenia   49

5   Learning and memory   51

5.1   Single vs double dissociations   52
5.2   Graphical representation of how memory strength and prediction error progress during learning   53
5.3   Progression of memory-related properties in the ventral visual pathway   54
5.4   Conversion of short-term memory into long-term memory   55
5.5   Associative LTP   56
5.6   Increasing output via LTP   57
5.7   Increasing output via LTD   58
5.8   The hippocampus   59
5.9   Systems consolidation   60
5.10 Multiple trace theory   61
5.11 Neural circuitry of memory extinction   62

6   Sensory systems   65

6.1   Components of the eye   66
6.2   The eye captures light   67
6.3   The retina   68
6.4   Cone and rod receptors   70
6.5   Retinal ganglion receptive fields   71
6.6   The visual pathway   72
6.7   The ventral and dorsal visual pathways   73
6.8   The auditory system   74
6.9   The cochlea   75
6.10 Diagram of the auditory pathway   77
6.11 The vestibular system   78
6.12 The utricle and saccule   79
6.13 The main types of touch receptor in the skin   80
6.14 The dorsal column-medial lemniscal (DCML) pathway   81
6.15 The descending pain inhibition circuit   83
6.16 Taste pathway from tongue to brain   84
6.17 Taste bud   86
6.18 Olfaction   87
6.19 The main olfactory pathway   89

7   Motor control   91

7.1   Muscles of the upper arm   92
7.2   The neuromuscular junction   93
7.3   Muscle fibre contraction   94
7.4   The spinal stretch reflex   95
7.5   Main brain areas involved in motor control   96
7.6   The basal ganglia   97
7.7   The cerebellum   98
7.8   Cross section through the cerebellar cortex   99

8 Emotional behaviours — 101

8.1 Schematic representation of the James-Lange theory of emotion — 102
8.2 Schematic representation of the Cannon-Bard theory of emotion — 103
8.3 Schematic representation of the Schachter-Singer theory of emotion — 104
8.4 Representation of the limbic system — 105
8.5 Core emotional facial expressions — 106
8.6 The hypothalamic-pituitary-adrenal axis — 107

9 Motivated behaviours — 109

9.1 Digestive system — 110
9.2 Hypothalamic nuclei involved in eating — 111
9.3 Affective reactions to taste — 112
9.4 The mesolimbic and mesocortical dopamine system — 113
9.5 EEG patterns observed during waking and sleep — 114
9.6 Sleep stages during one night — 115
9.7 Brain areas involved in waking — 116
9.8 Brain areas involved in sleep — 117
9.9 A schematic of the flip-flop mechanism that controls shifts between sleeping and waking — 118

Answers — 119

WHY CHOOSE A COLOURING BOOK FOR LEARNING BIOLOGICAL PSYCHOLOGY?

- Incorporates a different style of learning
- Creates a visual relationship with the content
- Improves your ability to remember and recall the content
- Provides a fun alternative/addition to traditional learning

Colouring is not just a fun way to unwind or a passing mindfulness fad, it actually has a number of beneficial properties making it the perfect complement to your studies. Firstly, it helps incorporate a different style of learning into your studies, helping you break from the traditional methods and try something new and fun. It also creates a visual relationship with the content, helping you to remember and recall the content as needed for your assignments and exams. Lastly, it can also improve your understanding, setting you up successfully not only for your Biological Psychology modules here and now, but also for the rest of your degree and beyond, whatever path you may choose.

HOW TO USE THIS BOOK

This book has been designed to take you through most of the core topics you will study as part of your Biological Psychology course. Throughout the book you will be able to:

- Revise key content using short introductions
- Work through each image using the instructions provided
- Label and mark up images to help test your knowledge
- Colour in each image to solidify your understanding!

To get the most out of this book you will need a full set of colouring pencils; a standard pack of 24 should include every colour you'll need. Answers to the labelling activities can be found at the end of the book.

We hope you enjoy using this book and it helps you as you develop your understanding and knowledge of Biological Psychology.

'I found this a helpful way to shift gears from reading a textbook but remain focused on consolidating knowledge. It would make an excellent companion to learning and revision.'

Nick Sherratt, University of Chester, MSc Psychology (Conversion)

Front cover endorsement from Niamh Hunniford, studying BSc Psychology at the University of Chester

ABOUT THE AUTHORS

Professor Suzanne Higgs has a degree in Psychology, Philosophy and Physiology from the University of Oxford, UK. During her degree she became fascinated by the effects of drugs on the brain and behaviour, which motivated her to pursue a PhD in Psychopharmacology at the University of Durham. After her PhD, she worked as a Postdoctoral researcher at the University of Oxford before moving to the University of Birmingham, UK to take up a faculty position in the School of Psychology. She has taught at all levels on the BSc in the Psychology programme at Birmingham and has over 20 years of lecturing experience. She specialises in teaching psychopharmacology and the biological bases of motivated behaviours, in particular, the psychobiology of appetite, which is the topic of her research.

Dr Alison Cooper's interest in Neuroscience began during her Natural Sciences degree when she accidentally found herself studying the properties of neurons that form the circuit that controls grasshopper movement. She pursued an interest in understanding how activity of neuronal cells could underpin behaviour for her PhD by researching the properties and functions of the parts of the brain that contribute to human motor behaviour. During this time, she became interested in neuropharmacology, and the link between synaptic neurotransmission and human function/dysfunction has remained the focus of her thoughts. Following various Postdoctoral positions, she took an ever-greater role in Neuroscience education of undergraduates on various professional and non-professional undergraduate programmes. In recent years she has used her experience to extend her interest in education to the general public who want to understand their own or others' brains through public engagement in person and, globally, through online courses.

Dr Jonathan Lee has a degree in Natural Sciences, specialising in Neuroscience, from the University of Cambridge. He has always been interested in the value of studying biological mechanisms in order to understand behaviour. This interest has been particularly focused on unconscious memories and their impact upon behaviour. In his PhD and Postdoctoral research, also at the University of Cambridge, he studied the contribution of gene expression and pharmacological mechanisms in the processes underlying long-term fear and addictive drug memories. He has continued these research interests since moving to the University of Birmingham, using his research experience to teach an introduction to Biological Psychology in the BSc Psychology programme.

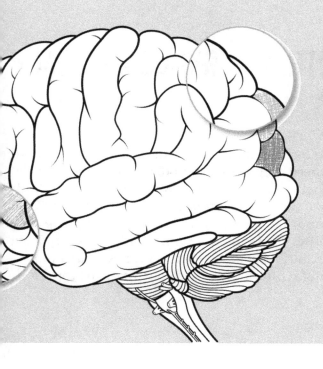

CHAPTER 1

STRUCTURE OF THE NERVOUS SYSTEM

INTRODUCTION

The relationship between biology and psychology is predominantly focused on the function of the nervous system (particularly the brain) in underpinning normal and abnormal behaviour. Therefore, a full understanding of biological psychology necessitates starting with the structure of the nervous system. Although the brain is the key part of the nervous system for determining human behaviour, before we can consider the function/dysfunction of the brain we need to have some understanding of how the whole human nervous system is organised and the role that the rest of the nervous system plays in both providing the brain with information and also carrying out actions determined by it. This chapter will help you understand and review the basic structures of the nervous system. Remember to review Chapter 2 of *Biological Psychology*.

Answers to the labelling exercises can be found at the back of the book.

1.1 THE PERIPHERAL AND CENTRAL NERVOUS SYSTEM

INTRODUCTION

Although the brain is the key part of the nervous system for determining human behaviour, before we can consider the function/dysfunction of the brain we need to have some understanding of how the whole human nervous system is organised and the role that the rest of the nervous system plays in both providing the brain with information and also carrying out actions determined by it. Traditionally, the nervous system is divided into two major parts: the central nervous system (CNS) and the peripheral nervous system (PNS). The central nervous system comprises the brain and spinal cord, and everything else is considered the peripheral nervous system. This terminology arose from centuries of anatomical studies where observation suggested that the brain and spinal cord gave rise to thin string-like projections which went all over the body.

────── **COLOURING NOTES 1.1** ──────

Label and colour:

- ☐ Brain
- ☐ Spinal cord
- ☐ Nerves
- ☐ Central nervous system (yellow)
- ☐ Peripheral nervous system (red)

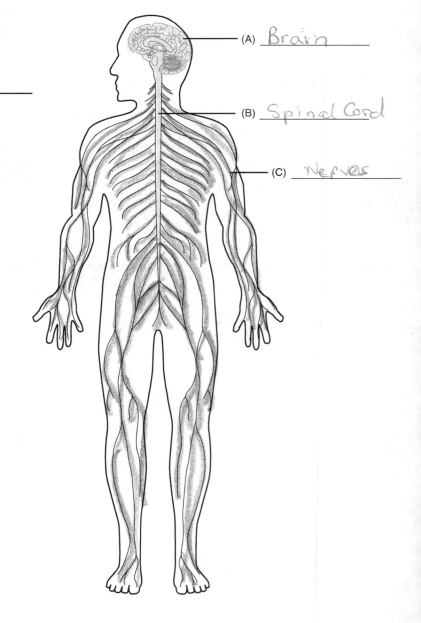

(A) _Brain_

(B) _Spinal Cord_

(C) _Nerves_

1.2 ANATOMICAL DIRECTIONS

INTRODUCTION

Table 1.1 shows the terms used to indicate the relative positions of the organs and parts of the body. The body can be divided by three lines:

- Horizontal: into superior (upper/above) and inferior (lower/below)
- Sagittal: into right and left halves either side of the median line
- Coronal: into anterior (front half) and posterior (back half)

The same terminology is also often applied to the brain.

Ventral/ anterior	Front of the body	Dorsal/ posterior	Back of the body
Superior	Above	Inferior	Below
Medial	Towards the midline	Lateral	Away from the midline
Proximal	Closer to point of origin or body	Distal	Further from point of origin or body
Superficial	Closer to body surface	Deep	Further from body surface

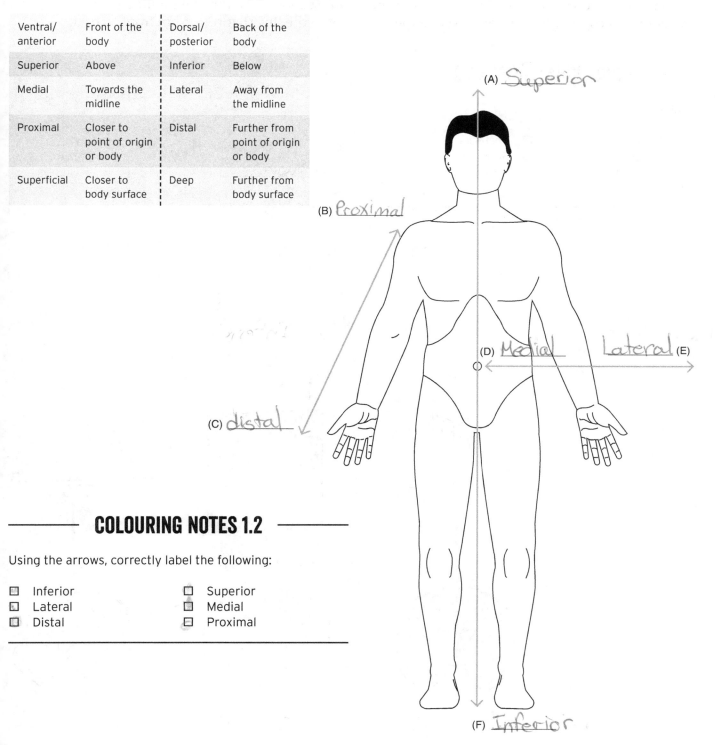

(A) Superior
(B) Proximal
(C) distal
(D) Medial
(E) Lateral
(F) Inferior

——— COLOURING NOTES 1.2 ———

Using the arrows, correctly label the following:

- ☑ Inferior
- ☑ Lateral
- ☐ Distal
- ☐ Superior
- ☑ Medial
- ☑ Proximal

1.3 TERMS USED TO INDICATE DIRECTION AND ORIENTATION IN THE NERVOUS SYSTEM

INTRODUCTION

The terms used to specify location in the central nervous system are the same as those used for the gross anatomical description of the rest of the body, e.g. anterior and posterior (or rostral and caudal) indicate front and back; superior versus inferior (or dorsal and ventral), top and bottom; and medial and lateral, the midline or away from the midline. The assignment of these anatomical axes then dictates the standard planes for histological sections or images used to study the brain anatomy. Horizontal sections are taken parallel to the superior/inferior axis of the brain. Sections taken in the midline plane are sagittal sections and coronal sections are taken perpendicularly to the line that runs from front to back.

—————— **COLOURING NOTES 1.3** ——————

Label:

- ☐ Coronal section
- ☐ Sagittal section
- ☐ Horizontal section
- ☑ Anterior
- ☑ Posterior
- ☑ Superior inferior arrow

(B) Superior inferior

(A) Anterior

(C) Posterior

(D) Inferior

(E) Coronal

(F) Sagittal

(G) Horizontal

The BioPsychology Colouring Book, published 2021 by SAGE Publishing. © Suzanne Higgs, Alison Cooper and Jonathan Lee, 2021

1.4 KEY FEATURES OF THE HUMAN BRAIN

INTRODUCTION

The brain is the largest structure in the human body to be almost entirely encased in a hard, bony structure, the skull, which indicates a critical need to protect it from damage. Visual inspection of the intact human brain shows that it consists of three distinct parts: (1) a stalk which joins the brain to the spinal cord, known as the brainstem; (2) a large domed structure of uniform appearance (if folded) known as the cerebrum; and (3) a smaller version of the cerebrum, found at the back and tucked in underneath the cerebrum, known as the cerebellum. When viewed from above we can see that the cerebrum consists of two mirror-image halves known as hemispheres. If a cut is made along the midline of the hemispheres and the cut surface viewed, it is clear that each hemisphere consists of the folded outer surface, known as the cerebral cortex, but also a collection of structures beneath the cortex which are not visible in the intact brain; these structures are collectively known as subcortical regions.

———— COLOURING NOTES 1.4 ————

Label and colour:

☐ Brainstem (green)
☐ Cerebellum (purple)
☐ Right and left cerebral hemispheres (orange)

Note, one of these labels applies to both images.

BACK

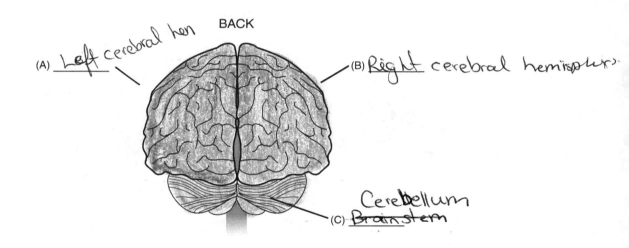

(A) _Left cerebral hen_

(B) _Right cerebral hemisphere_

Cerebellum
(C) _Brainstem_

MIDSAGITTAL

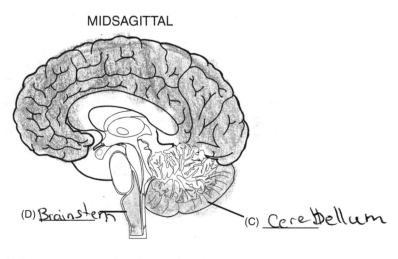

(D) _Brainstem_

(C) _Cerebellum_

1.5 THE LOBES OF THE BRAIN

INTRODUCTION

Observation of a large number of human brains resulted in the finding that some of the fissures, known as sulci (singular: sulcus), that result from the folding of the cerebrum, can be identified readily in the brains from many individuals. It followed that the cerebral cortex could be subdivided into regions based on their location relative to these sulci. These regions are known as lobes and this terminology is often used in relation to particular functions.

COLOURING NOTES 1.5

Label and colour:

- ☑ Temporal lobe (grey)
- ☑ Brainstem (orange)
- ☑ Spinal cord (brown)
- ☑ Cerebellum (pink)
- ☑ Occipital lobe (green)

- ☑ Parietal lobe (yellow)
- ☑ Frontal lobe (blue)
- ☑ Central sulcus
- ☑ Lateral fissure

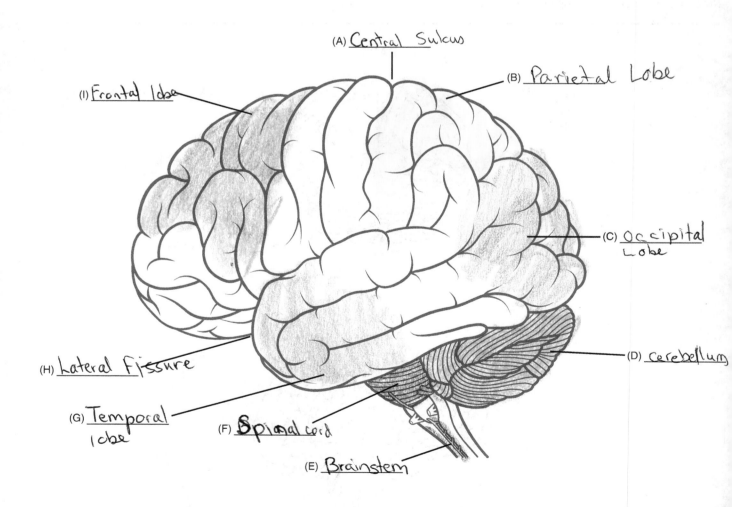

(A) Central Sulcus
(B) Parietal Lobe
(I) Frontal lobe
(C) Occipital Lobe
(D) Cerebellum
(H) Lateral Fissure
(G) Temporal lobe
(F) Spinal cord
(E) Brainstem

1.6 THE BRAINSTEM

INTRODUCTION

The brainstem joins the brain to the spinal cord. It consists of the medulla oblongata and pons, which make up the hindbrain, and the midbrain.

─────────────── **COLOURING NOTES 1.6** ───────────────

Label and colour:

☐   Midbrain (pink)
☐   Hindbrain
☐   Pons (purple)
☐   Medulla (blue)

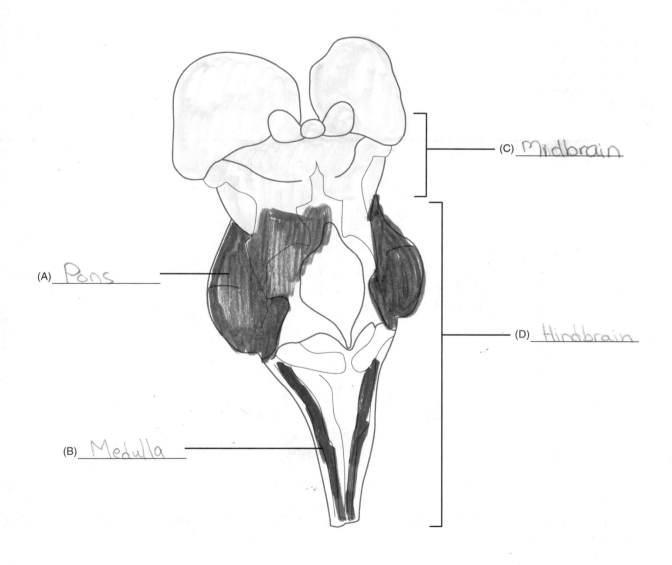

(A) Pons

(B) Medulla

(C) Midbrain

(D) Hindbrain

1.7 SLICE OF THE SPINAL CORD WITH SPINAL NERVES

INTRODUCTION

The spinal cord is a tube-shaped structure that runs from the base of the brain down through a series of bony rings known as vertebrae. Spinal nerves leave the spinal cord and exit via gaps between the vertebrae. The spinal nerves are collections of individual neuronal cells bundled together and as they travel away from the CNS they give rise to the extensive network of neural cells that travel to the extremities, allowing the CNS to communicate with the various organs and tissues all over the body. This information flows in both directions, that is, both towards and away from the CNS. As a general rule, where information is flowing towards the CNS, we term this **afferent** or sensory activity. Where information is flowing away from the CNS, we term this **efferent** or secretomotor activity.

──────── COLOURING NOTES 1.7 ────────

Label and colour:

☐ Soma of sensory neuron (blue)
☐ Soma of motor neuron (red)
☐ White matter
☐ Grey matter (grey)
☐ Dorsal root (pale blue)
☐ Ventral root (pink)
☐ Spinal nerve (green)
☐ Efferent
☐ Afferent

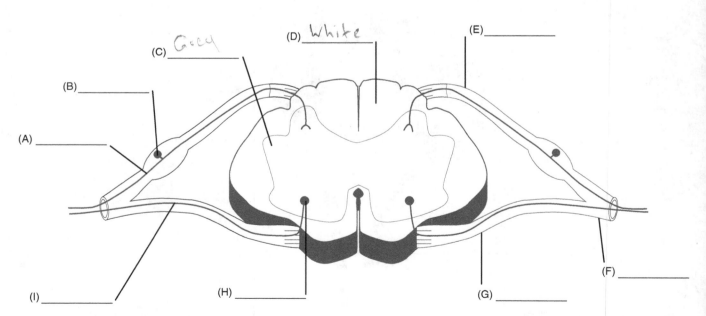

Adaptation based on Dr Jennifer Tobin's illustration for the Accelerated Cure Project at www.acceleratedcure.org/msresources/neuroanatomy

1.8 THE VENTRICLES OF THE BRAIN

INTRODUCTION

The ventricles of the brain are four cavities that contain cerebrospinal fluid (CSF) that supplies nutrients to the brain. The two lateral ventricles are found in the cerebral hemispheres (one in each hemisphere). They are connected to the third ventricle which is a narrow cavity that runs along the midline of the brain. The third ventricle is connected to the fourth ventricle via the cerebral aqueduct. The fourth ventricle connects with the central canal of the spinal cord.

--- **COLOURING NOTES 1.8** ---

Label and colour:

☐ Lateral ventricles (green)
☐ Third ventricle (blue)
☐ Fourth ventricle (purple)
☐ Cerebral aqueduct (red)
☐ Central canal of the spinal cord (yellow)

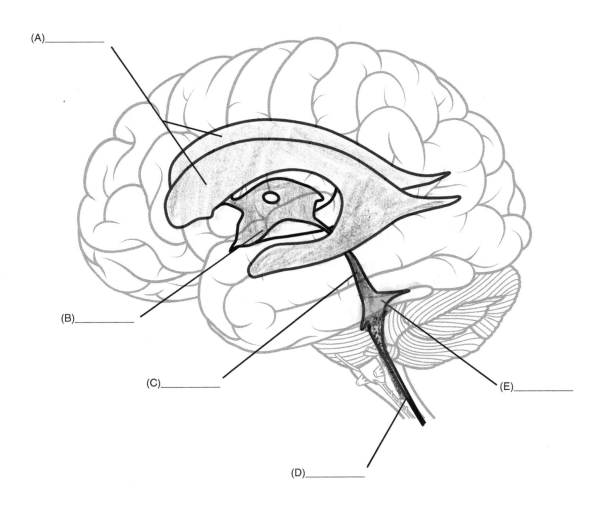

(A)_____

(B)_____

(C)_____

(D)_____

(E)_____

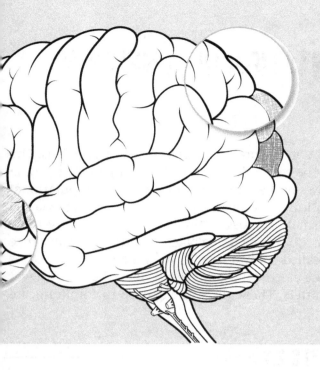

CHAPTER 2

COMMUNICATION IN THE NERVOUS SYSTEM

INTRODUCTION

The brain contains two types of specialised cell: neurons and glia. Neurons are the computational units that process information and initiate a response. Their cellular structure has evolved to optimise integration of information and communication with other cells. The major types of glia found in the human brain are oligodendrocytes, astrocytes and microglia. Originally it was considered that glia had a rather passive role, providing physical and metabolic support to the neurons. However, in recent years it has been recognised that the glia play a more important role than had previously been realised in enabling normal neuronal activity. The ability of neurons to communicate extensively with each other using electrochemical signalling processes, coupled with the ability at a cellular level for the intimate connections between neurons to subtly change, allows the human brain to be constantly adapting to our environment. This chapter will help you review the fundamentals of communication within the nervous system. Remember to review Chapter 2 of *Biological Psychology*.

Answers to the labelling exercises can be found at the back of the book.

2.1 TRADITIONAL REPRESENTATION OF A NEURON

INTRODUCTION

In common with most cell types, neurons contain the DNA of the individual, enveloped in a nucleus. The region of neurons where the nucleus is found is known as the cell body or soma. Projecting from the soma are a variable number of thin processes known as dendrites and axons. The result of the computational activity in the soma in response to the incoming information from the dendrites leaves the soma via the axon as an electrical signal. Axons, although extremely small in cross-sectional area, can be very long. Many of the axons of the peripheral nervous system (PNS) are wrapped in a pale-coloured lipid substance called myelin which is produced by a type of glial cell called Schwann cells. At the ends of the axons are the appropriately named synaptic terminals – once the electrical signals reach here, they can trigger the release of chemical substances known as neurotransmitters. These allow one neuron to communicate with other neurons to form a network.

— **COLOURING NOTES 2.1** —

Label and colour:

- ☐ Dendrites (purple)
- ☐ Cell body (purple)
- ☐ Nucleus (green)
- ☐ Axon (blue)
- ☐ Myelin sheath (yellow)
- ☐ Schwann cell nucleus (pink)
- ☐ Axon terminals (red)

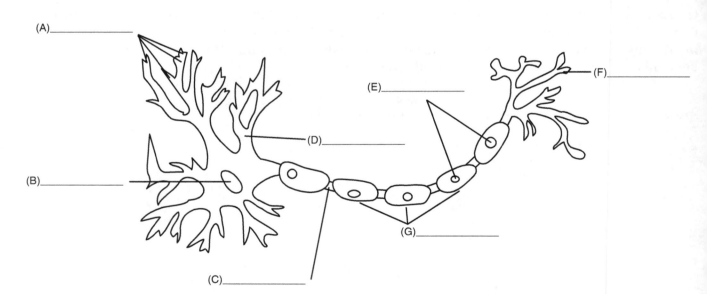

Adapted image based on: Quasar Jarosz/Wikimedia Commons. Shared under the CC BY-SA 3.0 license.

2.2 OLIGODENDROCYTES (GLIAL CELLS)

INTRODUCTION

Oligodendrocytes and Schwann cells are the glial cells that have a critical role in enabling axons to transmit electrical signals. Oligodendrocytes perform this role in the central nervous system and Schwann cells perform this role in the peripheral nervous system. It is these cells that produce the myelin that gives white matter its colour. The oligodendrocytes and Schwann cells wrap themselves around the axon, resulting in the myelin sheath which is formed of multiple layers of cell membrane. A single oligodendrocyte provides myelin for multiple segments of the axon and a Schwann cell covers one segment of an axon. Because the neuronal cell membrane is made of lipid and as such is electrically insulating, the electrical signals that travel down the axons are forced to jump between regions of axons which are not ensheathed by myelin, known as nodes of Ranvier, which increases the speed that the electrical signals can travel along the axon. Oligodendrocyte dysfunction and demyelination have been linked to conditions such as multiple sclerosis.

COLOURING NOTES 2.2

Label:

☐   Node of Ranvier
☐   Myelin sheath

Label and colour:

☐   Axon (yellow) N.B. this will need to be labelled twice on the diagram so make sure you find both places it appears!
☐   Schwann cell (purple)
☐   Oligodendrocyte (orange)

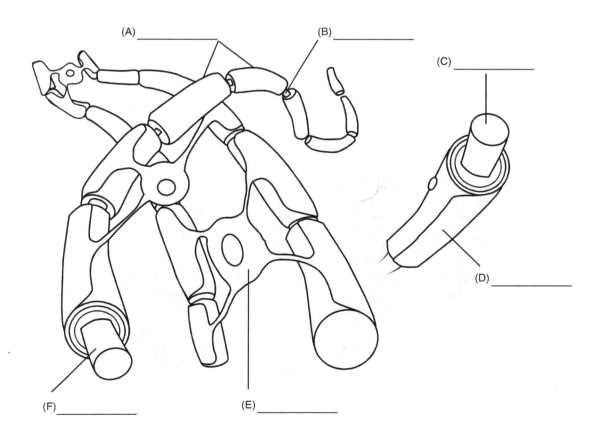

(A) _____   (B) _____   (C) _____

(D) _____

(F) _____   (E) _____

2.3 CROSS SECTION OF THE CELL MEMBRANE OF A NEURON

INTRODUCTION

To understand how neurons are able to transmit signals we need to know something about their structure. Neurons are bounded by a structure known as a cell membrane formed of various lipid-like substances and, for this reason, often described as the phospholipid bilayer. A consequence of this arrangement is that the phospholipid bilayer forms a physical barrier to the movement of substances in and out of the cell. The passage of these substances requires the presence of specific proteins which span the bilayer. One type of these proteins, called transporters, bind to substances and physically move them across the membrane. The other type is known as channels, which form pores allowing continuous contact between the extra- and intracellular environments. These channels and transporters play an important role in neuronal communication.

──────────────── COLOURING NOTES 2.3 ────────────────

Label:

☐ Extracellular fluid (outside neuron)
☐ Intracellular fluid (inside neuron)

Label and colour:

☐ Phospholipids (yellow)
☐ Protein channels (green)

(C)_____

(B) _____

(A) _____

(D) _____

2.4 A REPRESENTATION OF THE NEURONAL CELL MEMBRANE WITH A K+ CHANNEL AND THE NA+K+–ATPASE

INTRODUCTION

The properties of the neuronal membrane mean that large proteins, which act as anions as they carry a negative electrical charge, are 'trapped' within the intracellular fluid (cytosol). This has physiological consequences because both the extracellular fluid and the cytosol contain other charged entities, namely ions such as Na+, K+, and Cl–. However, the concentrations of these ions differ between the extra- and intracellular environments because of the continuous activity of the transporters. The most important transporter in this case is the Na+K+–ATPase, the activity of which produces a higher concentration of Na+ outside cells than in and the opposite situation for K+. This concentration difference means that these ions will tend to move down their concentration gradients through ion channels which are highly permeable to K+ and somewhat permeable to Na+. Another force that comes into play is the electrical attraction between the positively charged ions and the negatively charged proteins inside the cell. Eventually a point is reached whereby all these forces are balanced out and the resting membrane potential is reached.

———————————————————— **COLOURING NOTES 2.4** ————————————————————

Label:

☐ Outside neuron   ☐ Inside neuron

Label and colour:

☐ Na+ ions (red)   ☐ Phosolipids (yellow)
☐ Cl ions (light green)   ☐ K+ ion channel (green)
☐ K+ ions (blue)   ☐ Na+K+–ATPase transporter (orange)
☐ Anions (purple)

Note on labelling and colouring ions: colour ions labelled with an 'x' using the ion movement through the channel/transporter as a clue to the identity of the ion. For the other ions, consider the distribution and balance of ions between the inside and outside of the neuron and use this to guide your answers.

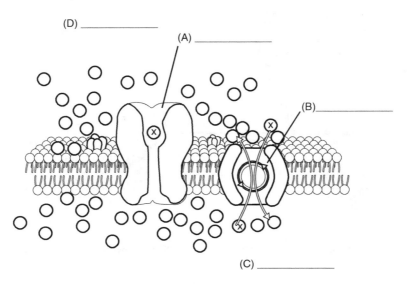

(D) _____

(A) _____

(B) _____

(C) _____

Garrett, B. (2011). *Brain and Behavior: An introduction to biological psychology.* Sage Publications, Inc.

2.5 THE ACTION POTENTIAL

INTRODUCTION

A key feature of neurons which underlies their ability to communicate is that they can change their membrane potential in response to a stimulus or message. This is because they can alter the ease with which ions can cross the membrane. Voltage-gated sodium channels and voltage-gated potassium channels are the critical components that allow the membrane potential to change and generate a self-perpetuating signal known as the action potential. It is these action potentials which allow the faithful transmission of a message from one end of the neuron to the other. At a membrane potential that is slightly more positive than that of the resting membrane potential, voltage-gated ion channels open and the ion flux through them contributes to changes in membrane potential (known as depolarisation), which promote further channel opening until the system becomes self-sustaining; this point is termed the threshold potential and once it is reached an action potential will occur. The depolarising phase is immediately followed by a repolarising phase when the membrane potential returns to a more negative state, ultimately attaining the resting membrane potential.

--- **COLOURING NOTES 2.5** ---

Label:

☐ Stimulus
☐ Depolarisation
☐ Repolarisation

Label and colour:

☐ Resting potential line (yellow)
☐ Threshold line (blue)

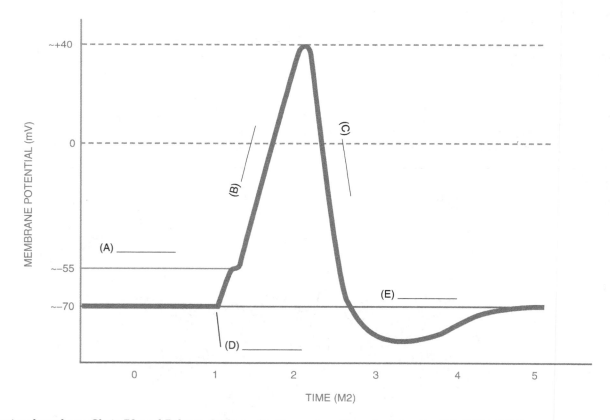

Adaptation based on: Chris 73 and Diberri, Wikimedia Commons. Shared under the CC BY-SA 3.0 license.

2.6 THE SYNAPSE BETWEEN A PRESYNAPTIC NEURON AND POSTSYNAPTIC NEURON

INTRODUCTION

Action potentials are the means by which signals are transmitted within a neuron but neurons communicate with each other and transmit signals between neurons. The term **synapse** is used to describe a structural arrangement comprising the cell providing the information and the cell receiving it. In fact, the 'input' and 'output' cells are named according to their position relative to the synapse. Hence, the cell bringing the information to the synapse is termed the *presynaptic* cell; the one that receives the information and acts as the output from the synapse is known as the *postsynaptic* cell. It is important to remember that postsynaptic cells may be neurons, the arrangement found in the brain, but may be other cell types such as skeletal or smooth muscle, as we find in the rest of the body. The gap between neurons is referred to as the synaptic cleft.

COLOURING NOTES 2.6

Label:

☐ Presynaptic neuron
☐ Postsynaptic neuron
☐ Synaptic cleft

Label and colour:

☐ Axon terminal (yellow)
☐ Dendrites (orange)
☐ Axons (purple)
☐ Presynaptic axon (blue)
☐ Postsynaptic axon (green)

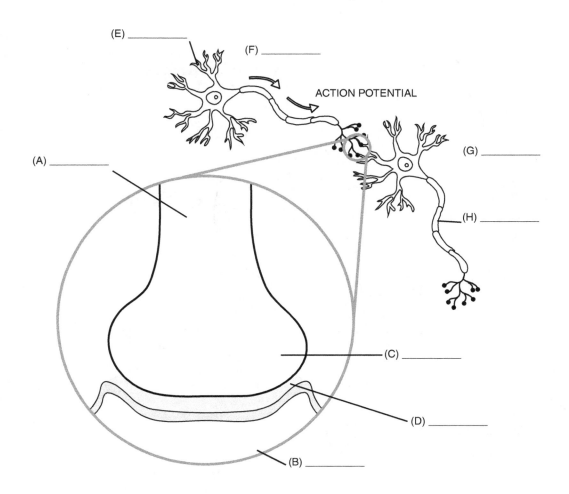

2.7 THE KEY STRUCTURES OF THE SYNAPSE

INTRODUCTION

If we study the structure of synapses, we see that they have some reproducible features. Within each of the terminals a large number of membrane-bound sacs, known as vesicles, can be seen and, under certain circumstances, these vesicles appear to fuse with the main plasma membrane. We now know that these vesicles contain chemical substances which can be released into the extracellular environment when vesicle fusion with the cell membrane occurs. The chemical substances that can be released in this way are chemically rather diverse and so are collectively known as neurotransmitters to reflect their function.

-------- **COLOURING NOTES 2.7** --------

Label and colour:

☐ Axon (orange)
☐ Synaptic vesicle (green)
☐ Synaptic cleft
☐ Dendrite (yellow)
☐ Neurotransmitter (green)

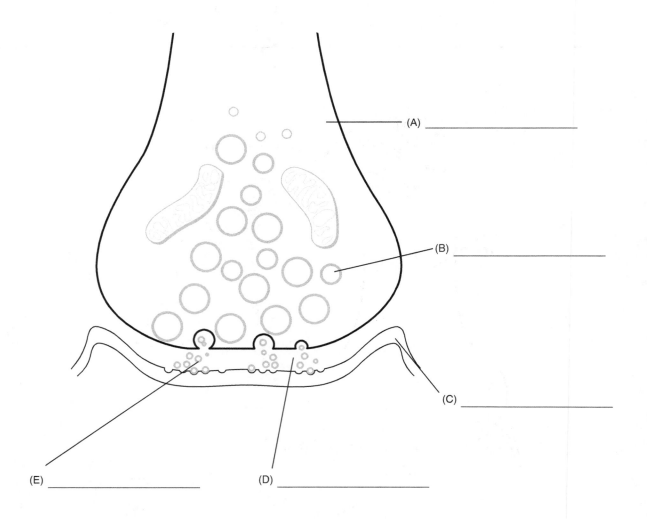

(A) _____

(B) _____

(C) _____

(E) _____   (D) _____

2.8 EXOCYTOSIS

INTRODUCTION

The process of releasing neurotransmitters into the synaptic cleft involves a process called exocytosis. Exocytosis involves the vesicles fusing with the neuronal membrane and releasing its contents into the synaptic cleft.

─────────────────── **COLOURING NOTES 2.8** ───────────────────

Label:

☐ The vesicle
☐ The synaptic cleft

Label and colour:

☐ Neurotransmitter molecules (orange)
☐ Cytoplasm (blue)

Draw an arrow to show the direction of movement between different stages in each image

(A)_____

(D)_____

(C)_____

(B)_____

2.9 POSTSYNAPTIC TRANSMISSION

INTRODUCTION

Release of the neurotransmitter into the synaptic cleft is of little consequence unless the postsynaptic cell can detect the presence of the neurotransmitter and initiate appropriate responses within the cell. Furthermore, the existence of multiple neurotransmitters suggests a degree of specificity; that is, that the postsynaptic cell should only respond to particular messages. This specificity is brought about by the existence of receptors on the postsynaptic cell which are highly specific to a particular neurotransmitter. Receptors are large protein molecules which are usually embedded within the phospholipid bilayer. These proteins have a highly developed structure which means that they can only interact with neurotransmitters of a particular shape. As a consequence, postsynaptic cells are only affected by the neurotransmitters for which they have the relevant receptors. One way in which neurotransmitters are removed from the synapse is via proteins that are embedded in the presynaptic neuron and transport neurotransmitters back into the presynaptic cell – a process known as reuptake.

COLOURING NOTES 2.9

Label:

☐ Axon terminal
☐ Synaptic cleft
☐ Dendrite
☐ Synaptic vesicle

Label and colour:

☐ Postsynaptic receptor (green)
☐ Neurotransmitter (blue)
☐ Neurotransmitter transporter (pink)

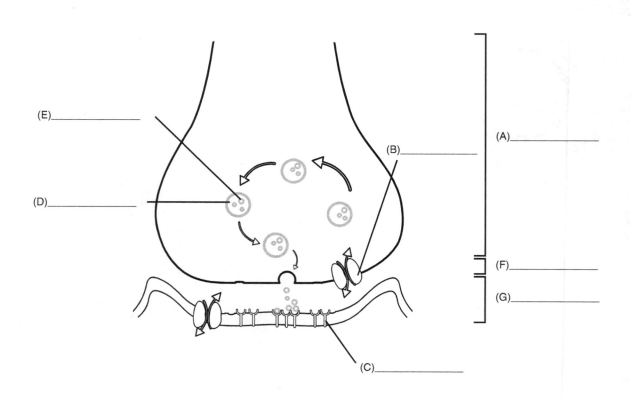

2.10 THE TRIPARTITE SYNAPSE

INTRODUCTION

Recent evidence suggests that glia play a role in determining synaptic levels of neurotransmitters. There is evidence that they can both take up and release transmitter substances, thus modulating the degree of synaptic transmission between the pre- and postsynaptic neurons. This research has resulted in the proposal of the concept of the tripartite synapse, composed of the presynaptic terminal, the postsynaptic dendrite and glial cells, specifically astrocytes. One of the emerging findings from these studies is that glial dysfunction may result in inappropriate neurotransmission.

───────────────────── **COLOURING NOTES 2.10** ─────────────────────

Label:

☐   Presynaptic terminal
☐   Synaptic cleft
☐   Postsynaptic terminal

Label and colour:

☐   Synaptic vesicle (red)
☐   Receptors (pink)
☐   Neurotransmitter (blue)
☐   Astrocyte (green)

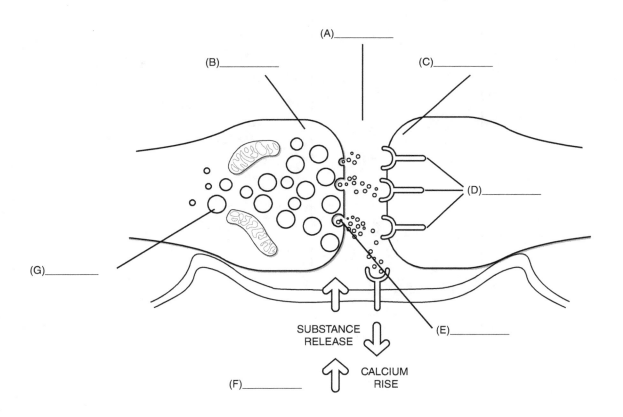

2.11 NEUROTRANSMITTERS

INTRODUCTION

Traditionally, neurotransmitters have been classified according to their chemical nature, for example if they are derivatives of amino acids. While this tells us little about their function, it does give us a way of grouping them systematically as either derivatives of amino acids, monoamines, neuropeptides, or lipid/gases.

COLOURING NOTES 2.11

Place the following neurotransmitters in their correct place in the table:

- ☐ GABA
- ☐ Serotonin
- ☐ Opioids
- ☐ Cannabinoids
- ☐ Glutamate
- ☐ Dopamine
- ☐ Neuropeptide Y

- ☐ Nitric oxide
- ☐ Glycine
- ☐ Histamine
- ☐ Orexin
- ☐ Noradrenaline
- ☐ Cholecystokinin

Amino Acids	Monoamines	Neuropeptides	Lipid/Gases

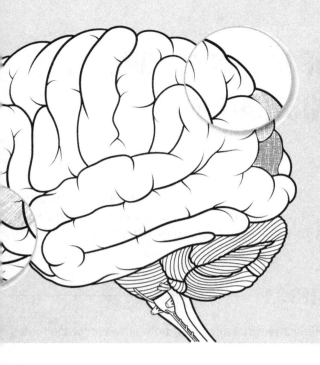

CHAPTER 3

DRUGS AND THE NERVOUS SYSTEM: PSYCHOPHARMACOLOGY

INTRODUCTION

Psychopharmacology is the study of psychoactive drugs and how they affect brain and behaviour. Psychoactive drugs are compounds that are not naturally present in the body but which can nevertheless act on the body to produce changes in mood and/or behaviour. Humans have taken drugs recreationally throughout history. Drugs bring about their effects on behaviour by altering neurotransmission. They enhance or dampen the effects of neurotransmitters. Stimulant drugs enhance dopamine and serotonin neurotransmission and increase arousal and alertness. Depressant drugs such as alcohol enhance GABA transmission and decrease glutamate transmission to inhibit neurotransmission. Other drugs such as psychedelics are taken for their ability to alter mood and perception. This chapter will help you review the effects of drugs on the nervous system. Remember to review Chapter 3 of *Biological Psychology*.

Answers to the labelling exercises can be found at the back of the book.

3.1 TIME COURSE OF ACTION OF DRUGS ACCORDING TO ROUTE OF ADMINISTRATION

INTRODUCTION

The time taken for a drug to bring about its effects on behaviour is determined in part by the route of administration. Some routes of administration are associated with faster drug onset than others. An important factor is whether a drug is administered directly into the bloodstream or whether it has to cross biological membranes to be absorbed.

———————————————— **COLOURING NOTES 3.1** ————————————————

Draw and label the relationship between brain concentration and time after drug administration for the following routes of administration:

☐ Inhalation in red
☐ Injection in blue
☐ Snorting/sniffing in orange
☐ Ingestion in green

CONCENTRATION OF DRUG IN BRAIN

TIME AFTER DRUG ADMINISTRATION

3.2 DOSE RESPONSE CURVE ILLUSTRATING ACTION OF AN AGONIST, ANTAGONIST AND INVERSE AGONIST

INTRODUCTION

The extent to which a drug activates a receptor is known as its efficacy. Antagonists have no efficacy because they do not induce a response in the receptor, whereas full agonists induce a response that is maximal relative to the effects of the neurotransmitter, and full inverse agonists induce a maximal response in the opposite direction. In between there are partial agonists and inverse agonists. These compounds activate receptors but even at very high doses the maximal response is not achieved.

COLOURING NOTES 3.2

Colour and label the following:

☐ Agonist: colour the markers red
☐ Antagonist: colour the markers green
☐ Partial inverse agonist: colour the markers blue

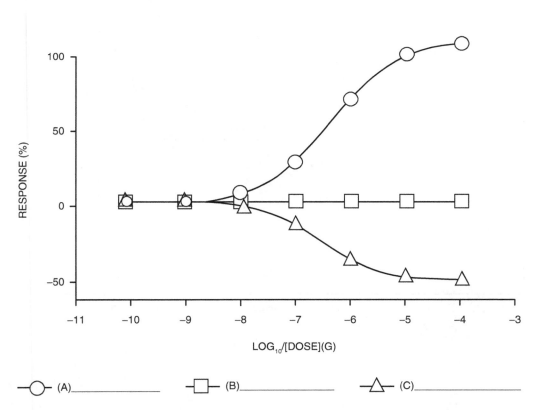

Reproduced from Lambert, D.G. (2004). 'Drugs and receptors', *Continuing Education in Anaesthesia Critical Care & Pain*, 4(6):181–184. With permission from Elsevier.

3.3 THE THERAPEUTIC INDEX

INTRODUCTION

The concept of therapeutic index refers to the relationship between a toxic and therapeutic dose. The therapeutic index determines the safety of a drug. Drugs with a large therapeutic index are preferred (a large difference between the toxic and clinical dose) because there is less likelihood of a person being able to overdose or experience toxic effects if they accidentally take too much of the drug.

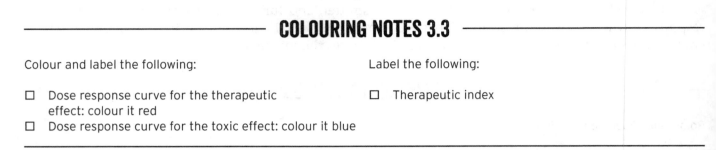

—————————— COLOURING NOTES 3.3 ——————————

Colour and label the following:

☐ Dose response curve for the therapeutic effect: colour it red
☐ Dose response curve for the toxic effect: colour it blue

Label the following:

☐ Therapeutic index

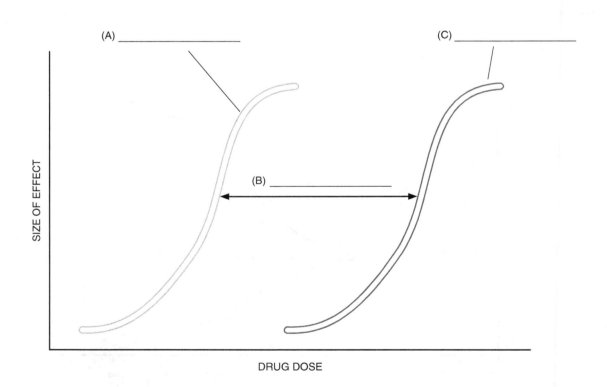

3.4 CHANGE IN DOSE RESPONSE CURVE WITH TOLERANCE AND SENSITISATION

INTRODUCTION

The acute effects of taking a psychoactive drug are often different from the effects that are experienced after a drug has been taken repeatedly. Neuronal systems adapt to drug-induced changes in neurotransmission. An adaptive response might be that numbers of receptors are down-regulated in response to increases in activation by drugs. This can lead to tolerance, whereby with repeated administration of drugs a higher dose is required to achieve the same effects. In other cases, the adaptive response is an increase in receptor numbers. This is known as sensitisation, meaning that the same dose of a drug elicits a greater response after repeated administration.

_____ **COLOURING NOTES 3.4** _____

☐ Relative to the acute dose response curve shown in the figure, identify and draw a dose response curve showing tolerance: draw it in purple
☐ Relative to the acute dose response curve shown in the figure, identify and draw a dose response curve showing sensitisation: draw it in green

_____

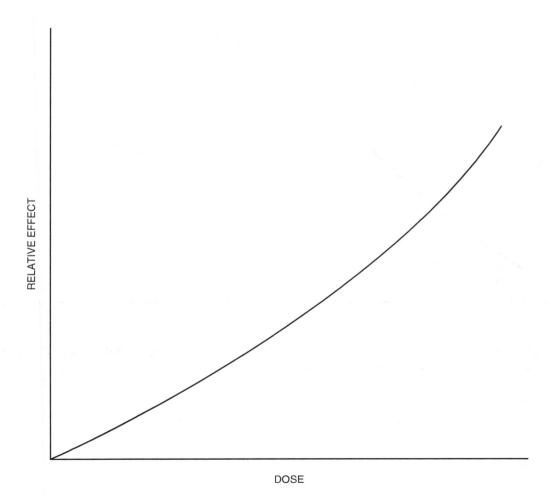

Adapted from Brunton, L. and Hilal-Dandan, R. (2014). *Goodman and Gilman's Manual of Pharmacology and Therapeutics*, second edition. New York: McGraw-Hill Education.

3.5 DOSE RESPONSE EFFECTS FOR ALCOHOL

INTRODUCTION

The effect of a drug depends upon the amount that is available at receptor sites. This is an important principle of drug action: drug effects are related to the dose of the drug. For example, very different effects of alcohol are experienced according to the dose administered.

COLOURING NOTES 3.5

On the dose response curve for alcohol in the figure, label the following behavioral effects along it:

☐ Sleep
☐ No effect
☐ Death
☐ Laboured breathing
☐ Giddy
☐ Unconscious

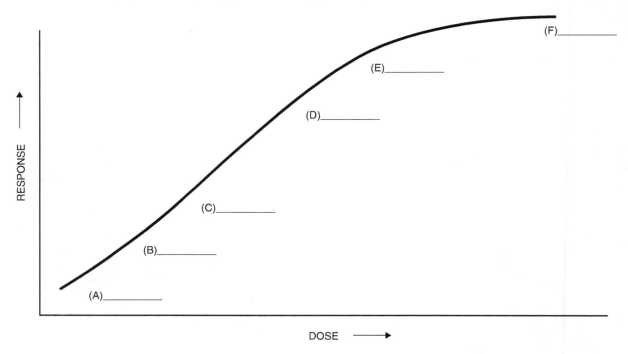

Adapted from Marczewski, A.E. and Kamrin, M. (1991) *Toxicology for the Citizen*, second edition. East Lansing, Mich: Michigan State University, Center for Integrative Toxicology. p.5.

3.6 IONOTROPIC AND METABOTROPIC RECEPTORS

INTRODUCTION

Drugs can affect neurotransmission by affecting the function of postsynaptic ionotropic and metabotropic receptors. Ionotropic receptors are membrane-bound receptor proteins that respond to ligand binding by opening an ion channel and allowing ions to flow into the cell, either increasing or decreasing the likelihood that an action potential will fire. Drug action at metabotropic receptors activates G-proteins, which then dissociate from the receptor and interact directly with ion channels or bind to other proteins that make intracellular messengers that open or close ion channels.

—— COLOURING NOTES 3.6 ——

Label the following across 3.6 (Part A) and 3.6 (Part B):

☐ Ionotropic receptor
☐ Metabotropic receptor
☐ Ion (and colour red)
☐ Closed ion channel
☐ Neurotransmitter (and colour blue)
☐ G-protein
☐ G-protein gated ion channel

Part A

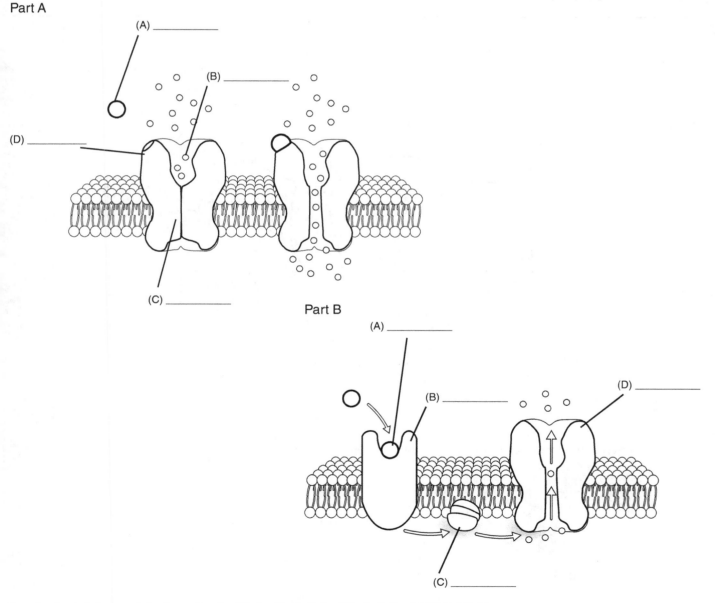

Part B

Part A adapted from original creation by Hrejsa/Body Scientific Intl. for SAGE Publishing

Part B adapted from original creation by Tomasikiewicz/Body Scientific Intl. for SAGE Publishing

3.7 THE GABA-A RECEPTOR COMPLEX

INTRODUCTION

Many drugs bring about their effects by acting at the GABA-A receptor complex, which is an ionotropic receptor. Some bind to a receptor site on the GABA-A receptor complex and directly increase the flow of Cl^- ions through the ion channel. Others bind to different receptor sites and have the effect of increasing the response to GABA binding at its site on the GABA-A receptor complex. These drugs are known as allosteric modulators.

─────────────── **COLOURING NOTES 3.7** ───────────────

☐ Identify three types of drug that interact with the GABA-A receptor and label each at a different receptor site on the GABA-A receptor complex
☐ Label and colour the GABA receptor site red
☐ Colour the Cl ions blue
☐ Label and colour the neural membrane yellow

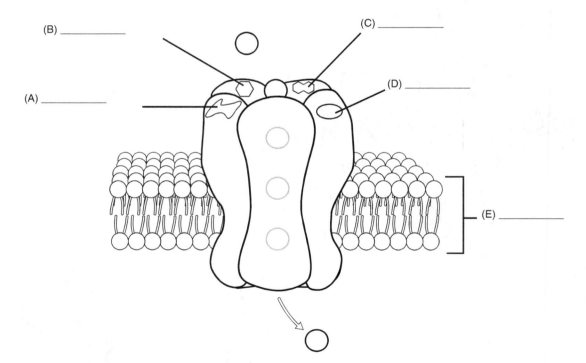

Adapted from original created by Carolina Hrejsa/Body Scientific Intl. for Sage Publishing.

3.8 EFFECTS OF COCAINE ON DOPAMINE NEUROTRANSMISSION

INTRODUCTION

Cocaine is a stimulant drug that when taken has short-term effects including increased alertness and a desire for further drug taking. Cocaine inhibits the reuptake of dopamine, serotonin and noradrenaline by binding to presynaptic transporter proteins, thus enhancing monoamine neurotransmission. The reinforcing effects of cocaine are likely mediated by its action to increase serotonin and dopamine transmission in reward pathways in the brain.

COLOURING NOTES 3.8

Label and colour the following:

- ☐ Dopamine (red)
- ☐ Presynaptic transporter protein (blue)
- ☐ Cocaine (orange)

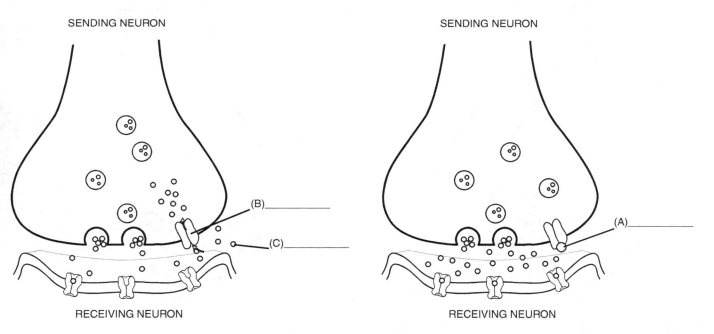

Adapted from original creation by Tomasikiewicz/Body Scientific Intl. for SAGE Publishing

3.9 EFFECTS OF MORPHINE ON OPIOID NEUROTRANSMISSION

INTRODUCTION

Opiates come from the poppy flower *Papaver somniferum*. Two opiates contained in poppy sap are morphine and codeine. The brain contains opioid receptors that bind opiate drugs and naturally occurring brain chemicals known as endogenous opioids. Opioid agonists such as morphine bring about similar effects to the endogenous opioids by binding to the endogenous opioid receptors.

─────────────── COLOURING NOTES 3.9 ───────────────

Colour and label the following:

☐   Endogenous opioids (green)
☐   Postsynaptic opioid receptor (orange)
☐   Morphine (yellow)

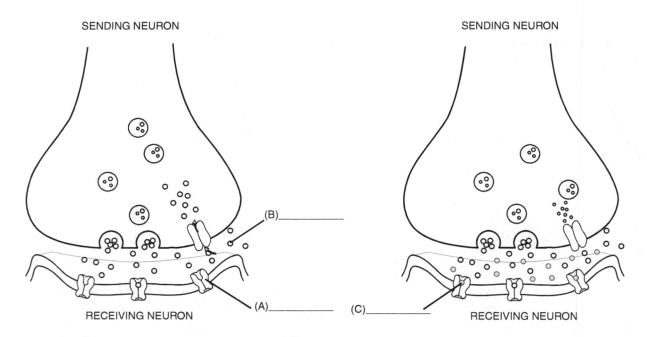

Adapted from original creation by Tomasikiewicz/Body Scientific Intl. for SAGE Publishing

3.10 THE ACTION OF NICOTINE IN THE BRAIN

INTRODUCTION

Nicotine is the drug found in cigarettes and other tobacco products such as chewing tobacco and snuff. Nicotine is an acetylcholine agonist and it binds to specific receptors called nicotinic acetylcholine receptors or nAChRs.

COLOURING NOTES 3.10

Colour and label the following:

- ☐ Acetylcholine (green)
- ☐ Nicotine (pink)
- ☐ Acetylcholine receptors (blue)
- ☐ Axon terminal

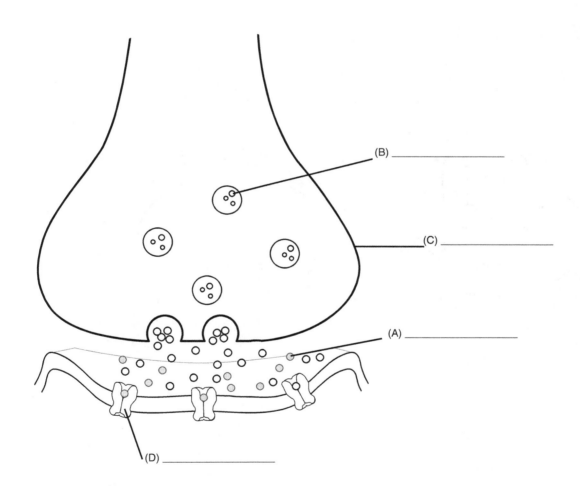

3.11 CAFFEINE BINDING TO ADENOSINE RECEPTORS

INTRODUCTION

Caffeine binds to adenosine receptors that are distributed throughout the body, including the brain. It is an adenosine antagonist. Generally speaking, the physiological effects of caffeine are the opposite to those of adenosine. For example, adenosine promotes sleep. When caffeine binds to adenosine receptors it prevents adenosine from binding and so has the effect of reducing sleep.

COLOURING NOTES 3.11

Colour and label the following:

- ☐ Caffeine (pink)
- ☐ Adenosine (green)

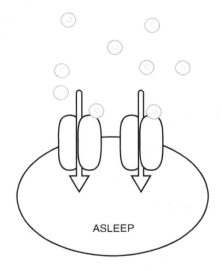

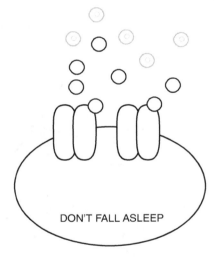

(A)_____

(B)_____

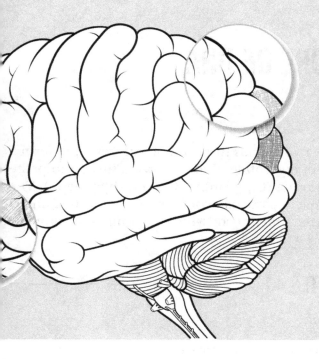

CHAPTER 4

DEVELOPMENT AND DEGENERATION IN THE NERVOUS SYSTEM

INTRODUCTION

The adult nervous system is composed of billions of cells, classified into two types: Neurons and glia. Yet all humans start out life as a single cell. Therefore, to build a functioning brain, there needs to be a complex and highly regulated process during development. This requires production of many billions of new cells and, for each one, the turning on and off of genes in the right sequence so that fully mature cells are produced in the right part of the brain and with the right complement of proteins to enable them to carry out their specialised functions. For neurons this means that they can form the synaptic connections with other neurons to form functional circuits known as networks. As for all biological tissues, cells can also die. When the level of neuron death is high this leads to degeneration of the nervous system and disruption to normal function. The consequence of this can be seen in human neurodegenerative disorders such as Parkinson's disease or Alzheimer's disease. Unfortunately, the natural capacity for neurons to be repaired or replaced is very limited. However, for some conditions, such as Parkinson's disease, therapeutic drugs can be used to make up for the impaired neuron function. Remember to review Chapter 4 of *Biological Psychology*.

Answers to the labelling exercises can be found at the back of the book.

4.1 THE STRUCTURE OF DNA

INTRODUCTION

Mammalian DNA is described as double-stranded and the two strands twist around each other to form a double helix shape. Each strand is made up of a sequence of nucleotides that comprise a sugar-phosphate backbone attached to one of four bases: adenine (A), cytosine (C), guanine (G), and thymine (T). The bases are described as complementary as they only combine in particular configurations: A with T and C with G. The sequence of the bases is important as it forms the genetic code which determines the proteins produced by cells.

COLOURING NOTES 4.1

Label:

☐ The sugar-phosphate backbone
☐ The complementary bases of the right hand strand

Colour:

☐ The left sugar-phosphate backbone light (grey)
☐ The right sugar-phosphate backbone (dark grey)
☐ The base adenine base (yellow)
☐ The base cytosine base (green)
☐ The base guanine base (red)
☐ The base thymine base (blue)

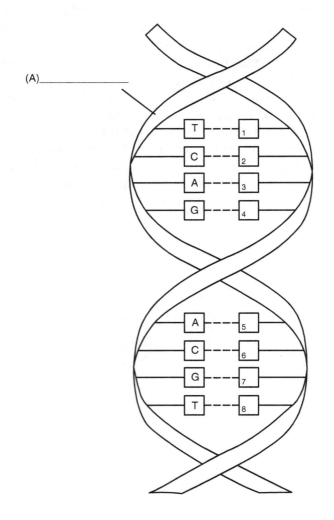

4.2 MEIOSIS AND MITOSIS

INTRODUCTION

Meiosis occurs in relation to reproduction and is the division that occurs to form the gametes – sperm or ova – in preparation for fertilisation and formation of the zygote which develops into the foetus. The gamete from each parent normally contains half the full number of chromosomes (i.e. 23:22 autosomes and one sex chromosome).

─────────────── **COLOURING NOTES 4.2** ───────────────

4.2(A)

Colour:

☐ The chromosomes (orange)
☐ Where the sister chromatids separate (red)
☐ The gametes (blue)
☐ The sister chromatids (yellow)
☐ Where the homologues separate
  (sisters remain attached) (green)

Label:

☐ Sisters separate
☐ DNA replication recombination
☐ Chromosome segregation (meiosis I)
☐ Homologues separate, sisters remain attached
☐ Homologous chromosome
☐ Sister chromatids
☐ Gametes
☐ Chromosome segregation (meiosis II)

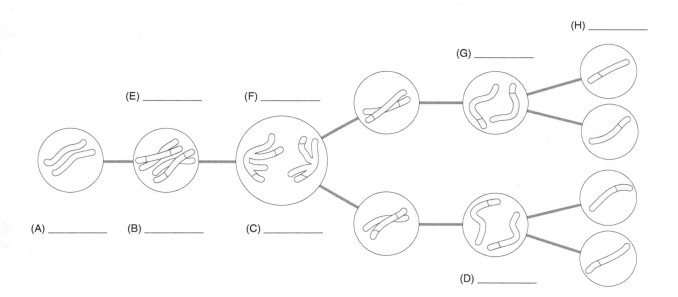

(A) _____ (B) _____ (C) _____ (D) _____ (E) _____ (F) _____ (G) _____ (H) _____

Mitosis is when a cell divides into two genetically identical daughter cells. Continued cell division occurs as the body develops through various stages. It also enables tissue repair.

Mitosis consists of five main stages (but not in this order):

- Telophase
- Metaphase
- Anaphase
- Interphase
- Prophase

4.2(B)

☐   Label the five phases of mitosis correctly on the diagram
☐   Colour the chromatids in the prophase and metaphase stages red
☐   Identify in which step the chromatids separate and colour them yellow
☐   Colour the chromosomes in the telophase stage green
☐   Colour the homologous chromosomes in the interphase stage orange

---

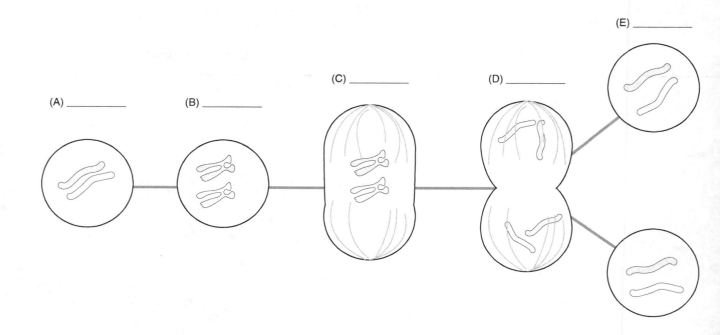

(A) _____   (B) _____   (C) _____   (D) _____   (E) _____

4.3 NEURULATION

INTRODUCTION

In early development, the fertilised egg undergoes a period of massive cell proliferation where repeated cell division results in a rapid increase in cell numbers within the embryo. Initially these cells appear to be virtually identical but in humans, by about week 3 after fertilisation, the uniform ball of cells has begun to take on shape and a layer of cells that are destined to produce the nervous system, called the ectoderm, can be identified; a process known as gastrulation. During the gastrulation phase the combination of differential gene expression and cell-to-cell interactions results in a process known as neural induction whereby a region of the ectoderm transforms into a structure known as the neural plate; as the name suggests this is the first sign that a nervous system will ultimately be formed. The embryo then enters the **neurulation** phase which begins with the embryo elongating and the formation of the neural plate from which the whole of the central nervous system arises.

─────────────────────── **COLOURING NOTES 4.3** ───────────────────────

Label:

☐ The neural plate
☐ The non-neural ectoderm
☐ The neural groove
☐ The neural tube

Colour:

☐ The non-neural ectoderm (blue)
☐ The regions of the ectoderm that will form the neural tube (beige)

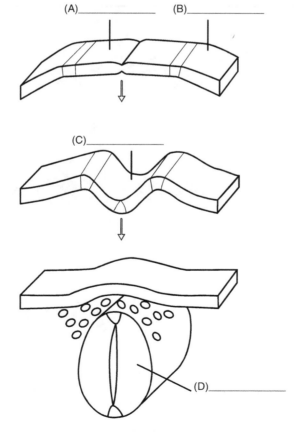

(A)_____ (B)_____

(C)_____

(D)_____

Adapted with permission from Liu, A. et al. (2005). 'Bone morphogenetic protein signalling and vertebrate nervous system development', *Nature Reviews Neuroscience.* Copyright Clearance Centre: Springer Nature.

4.4 THE BRAIN DEVELOPS FROM A TUBULAR STRUCTURE

INTRODUCTION

At the end of neurulation, the foetus contains a tubular structure that will go on to form the central nervous system. By 3–4 weeks after fertilisation, the anterior end of the tube that will form the brain and the posterior end that will form the spinal cord are evident. Over the next few weeks the region at the head end of the tube begins to expand due to on-going production of new cells. It also loses its simple tubular shape and starts to develop swellings, known as vesicles, which will go on to form the regions of the brain, such as the forebrain and midbrain which are all visible at birth.

——————————— COLOURING NOTES 4.4 ———————————

Colour and label:

☐   The forebrain at each time-point in development (red)
☐   The midbrain at each time-point in development (green)
☐   The hindbrain at each time-point in development (the cerebellum brown and the rest of the hindbrain yellow)

Label:

☐   Where the cranial nerves emerge from the hindbrain
☐   The spinal cord

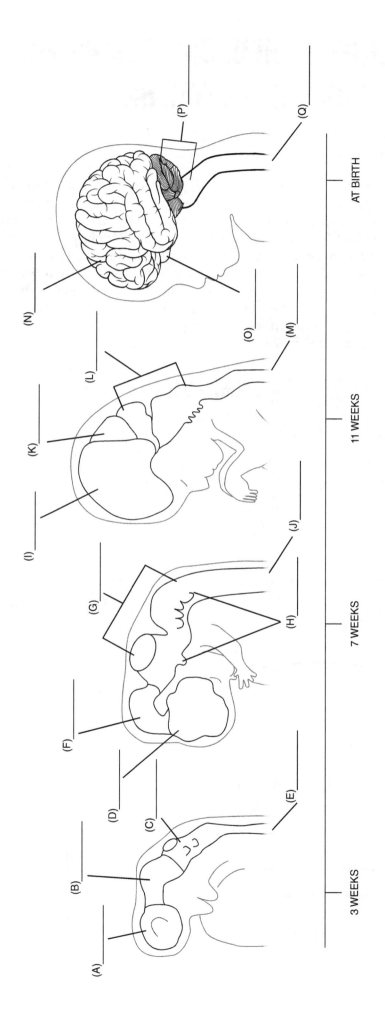

4.5 MIGRATION OF NEURONS DURING FORMATION OF THE FOETAL BRAIN

INTRODUCTION

Throughout early development there is a significant amount of proliferation of cells to enable enough neurons to be produced to form the brain. These newly produced neurons have to migrate from their place of production to the correct location within the forming brain. This migration process is particularly clear in the formation of the highly organised human neocortex which, when fully formed, is organised into layers of neurons with each layer containing neurons with slightly different shapes and connectivity to other neurons. Neurons are produced in the ventricular zone, a region that lines the fluid-filled space in the middle of the neural tube. They then need to migrate across the region that will ultimately form the full depth of the neortex, known as the cortical plate, towards the outer surface. This occurs in a very precise pattern whereby the first immature neurons migrate the shortest distance from the ventricular zone and subsequently produced immature neurons migrate further, a process termed inside-out layering.

COLOURING NOTES 4.5

Label:

☐ The fluid-filled ventricle
☐ The surface of the brain

Colour and label:

☐ The ventricular zone (brown)
☐ The cortical plate (pale blue)
☐ The radial glia (dark green)

Colour:

☐ The first-formed cortical neurons (yellow)
☐ Later formed neurons (pink)

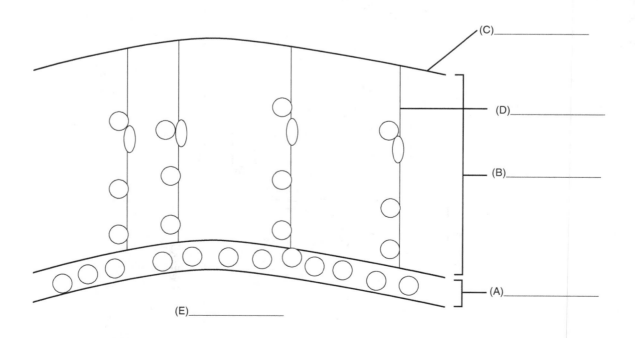

4.6 A NEURON MIGRATES ALONG GLIAL SCAFFOLDING

INTRODUCTION

Inside-out layering involves immature neurons migrating away from their place of birth in the ventricular zone to their final destination within the cortical plate. To do this they migrate along a scaffolding-like network of specialised glial cells known as radial glia.

COLOURING NOTES 4.6

Label:

☐ The ventricular zone
☐ The outer layer of the brain
☐ The migration zone
☐ Radial glial fibres
☐ Migrating neurons
☐ Outer layer of the brain (where the oldest neurons are)
☐ Ventricular zone (where the youngest neurons are)

Draw and colour:

☐ Colour the radial glia (dark green)
☐ Draw and colour a circle representing a first-formed neuron (yellow)
☐ Draw and colour later-formed neuron (pink)

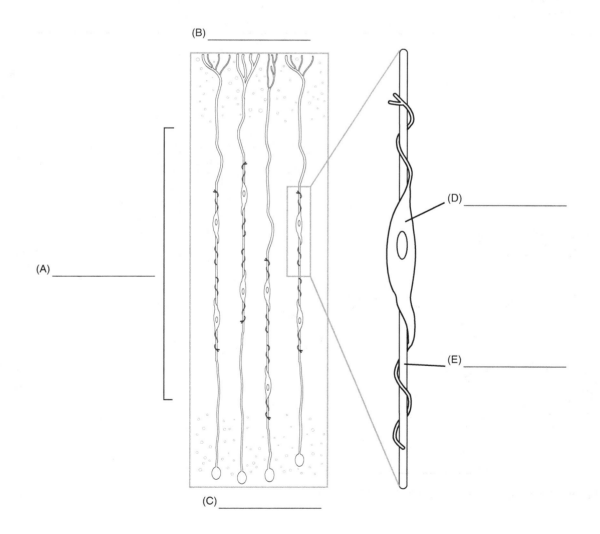

(B) _____

(A) _____

(C) _____

(D) _____

(E) _____

4.7 AXON GUIDANCE

INTRODUCTION

Fully differentiated neurons are characterised by having long extensions from their cell bodies, known as axons, which can allow an individual cell to communicate with other cells some distance away. Once immature neurons have been produced and have made it to the appropriate location within the developing brain they next need to extend their axons in the right direction to find their intended target neurons.

The process by which axons extend in the right direction is known as axon guidance and appears to involve the growing tip of the axon, known as a growth cone, 'tasting' the environment it is travelling through using receptor molecules which it expresses on its surface. The growth cone must also be highly mobile compared to the axon behind it and this difference is reflected in the proteins that form the cytoskeleton that acts as a kind of scaffolding within the neuron. Two of the components of the cytoskeleton are actin and microtubules.

COLOURING NOTES 4.7

Colour and label:

☐ The cell body (green)
☐ The axon (blue)
☐ The growth cone (red)

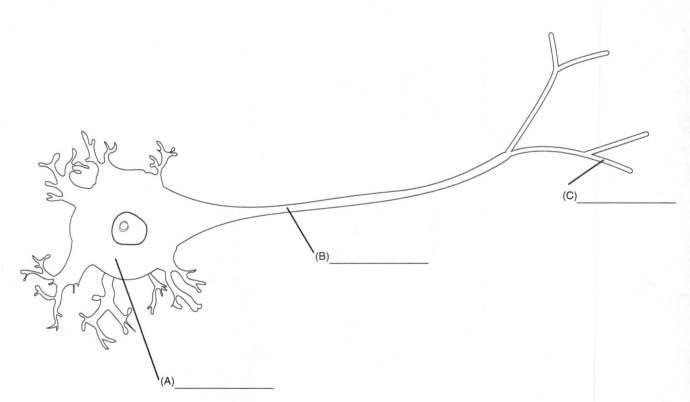

(C)_____

(B)_____

(A)_____

Adapted from illustration by Lydia Kibiuk, © 1995.

4.8 APOPTOSIS

INTRODUCTION

Apoptosis occurs in the brain during development and also occurs as part of some neurodegenerative disease in the adult brain. It is one of the two main processes by which cell death occurs, the other is called necrosis. Necrosis happens when cells are exposed to any form of accidental damage such as trauma or toxins. Apoptosis is a more controlled process involving proteins produced by the dying cells themselves in response to specific signals. For this reason it is sometimes known as programmed cell death. When a cell is undergoing apoptosis it passes through a number of stages with characteristic features.

─────────────── **COLOURING NOTES 4.8** ───────────────

Match these descriptions and label the correct diagram:

☐   Nuclear collapse
☐   Cell damage
☐   Cell parts phagocytosed
☐   Cell shrinks developing buds or blebs
☐   Cell breaks into apoptotic bodies
☐   Normal cell

☐   Colour the cytoplasm blue, the nucleus yellow, other cell organelles green

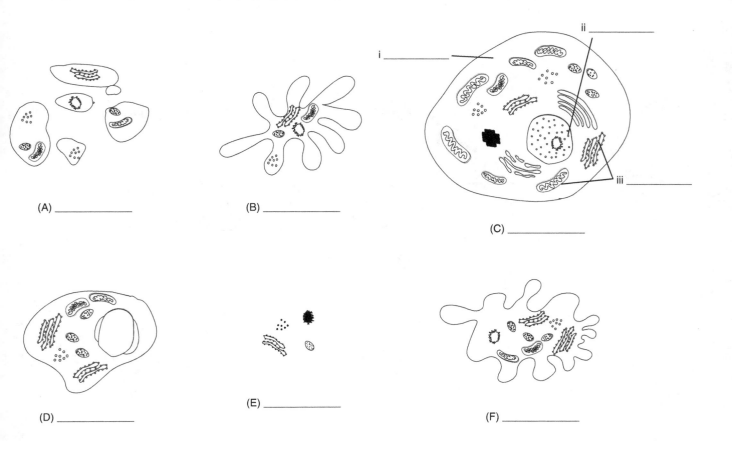

(A) _____

(B) _____

(C) _____

i _____

ii _____

iii _____

(D) _____

(E) _____

(F) _____

4.9 NEUROPATHOLOGY OF PARKINSON'S DISEASE

INTRODUCTION

Parkinson's disease is associated with characteristic neurodegeneration in a specific part of the brain called the substantia nigra pars compacta. It is called this because it has a black appearance due to the presence of melanin. The neurons in this region send their axons towards the caudate and putamen, collectively known as the striatum. This nigrostriatal pathway normally releases dopamine and this is important in regulating the activity in a brain circuit that controls normal movement.

COLOURING NOTES 4.9

Label:

☐ The healthy brain
☐ The brain in Parkinson's disease

Label and colour:

☐ The caudate and putamen (blue)
☐ The substantia nigra pars compacta (black)

Draw in:

☐ The nigrostriatal pathway in the healthy brain (solid red line)
☐ The nigrostriatal pathway of the brain with Parkinson's disease (a dashed red line)

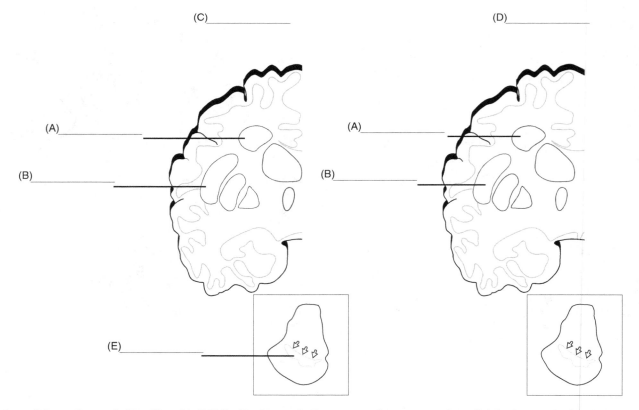

Adapted from Dauer & Przedborski (2003), 'Parkinson's Disease mechanisms and models', *Neuron*, 39(6): 889–909. With permission from Elsevier.

4.10 BRAIN WITH HUNTINGTON'S DISEASE

INTRODUCTION

Huntington's disease is associated with characteristic neurodegeneration of specific parts of the brain called the caudate and putamen. The neurodegeneration occurs because of a mutation in a single gene called huntington.

COLOURING NOTES 4.10

Label:

☐ The healthy brain
☐ The brain with Huntington's disease
☐ The caudate and putamen in the healthy brain

(C)_____

(D)_____

(A)_____

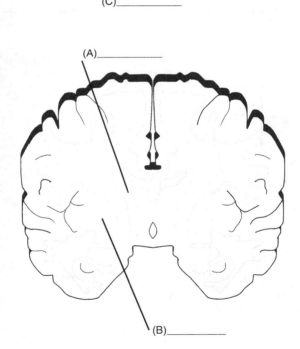

(B)_____

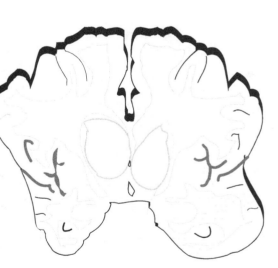

4.11 TREATMENT FOR PARKINSON'S DISEASE: L-DOPA

INTRODUCTION

Parkinson's disease is associated with degeneration of dopamine-producing neurons. The most common treatment seeks to replace the lost dopamine. In the body dopamine is made from L-DOPA which is made from tyrosine that is obtained from the diet. People with Parkinson's disease cannot take dopamine as it cannot cross the blood brain barrier. However, L-DOPA can cross the blood brain barrier and enter neurons where it is metabolised into dopamine that can be packaged for release from presynaptic terminals. This then restores better dopamine neurotransmission between the neurons of the substantia nigra and those of the caudate putamen and so movement is improved.

--- **COLOURING NOTES 4.11** ---

Colour and label:

☐ The presynaptic neuron (blue)
☐ The postsynaptic neuron (green)
☐ Vesicles containing dopamine (yellow)
☐ The synaptic cleft (no colour)
☐ Dopamine receptors (orange)

☐ Place these substances in the boxes in the order of synthesis: Dopamine, L-DOPA, tyrosine

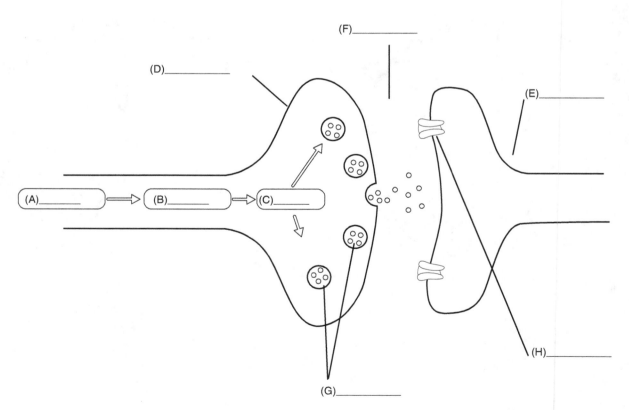

Adapted from Moussa B.H. Youdim et al. (2006). 'The therapeutic potential of monoamine oxidase inhibitors', *Nature Reviews Neuroscience.* Copyright Clearance Centre: Springer Nature.

4.12 GENES WITH NEUROTRANSMISSION RELATED FUNCTIONS IMPACTED IN SCHIZOPHRENIA

INTRODUCTION

Understanding the cause of human conditions that affect the brain and its functions has been a long-term goal. It is now clear that most conditions are complex, involving the interaction of environmental factors with the complement of genes that a person possesses. For such a complex condition as schizophrenia, detailed studies of the genes and the proteins that they produce have demonstrated that a large number of genes might be linked with the condition. For any one individual the precise versions, known as alleles, of a subset of the genes may predispose them to develop schizophrenia, especially if they have particular life experiences. Many of the genes that have been implicated for schizophrenia produce proteins that are important for normal neuronal function.

———————— COLOURING NOTES 4.12 ————————

- ☐ Colour the labelled boxes red
- ☐ For the 'receptors' box: Identify three types of neurotransmitter receptors implicated in schizophrenia. Colour the boxes green
- ☐ For the neurotransmitter levels box: Identify three processes that can be affected to alter the level of neurotransmitter. Colour the boxes red
- ☐ For each of the processes that alter neurotransmitter levels, identify at least one gene that has been linked to this process. Colour the boxes green

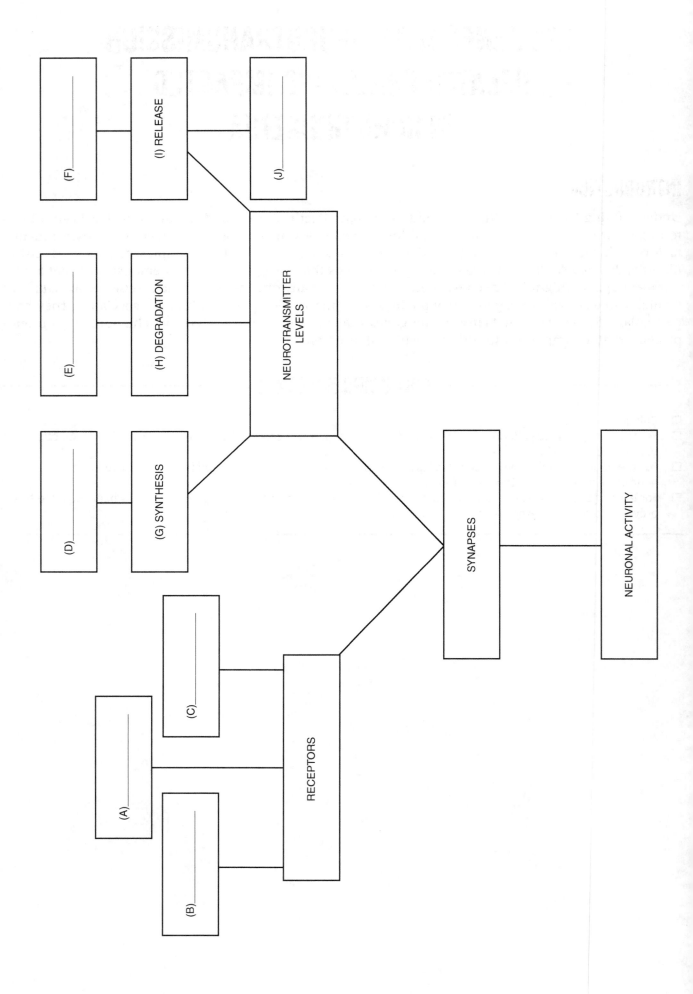

The diagram contains the following labeled boxes: (F), (I) RELEASE, (J), (E), (H) DEGRADATION, (D), (G) SYNTHESIS, NEUROTRANSMITTER LEVELS, (A), (C), (B), RECEPTORS, SYNAPSES, NEURONAL ACTIVITY

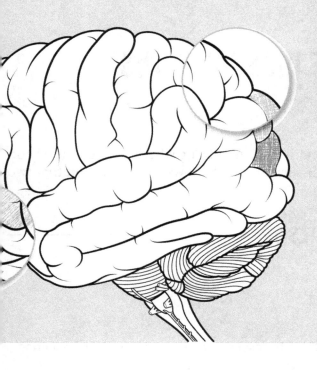

CHAPTER 5

LEARNING AND MEMORY

INTRODUCTION

Experiences alter our behaviour. The knowledge gained from a previous experience is stored as a memory that allows us to predict what might happen in the future. This happens for both conscious and unconscious memories, and there are multiple processes that take place from the time of learning to produce a long-lasting memory. This chapter will help you review some major processes and concepts in memory. Remember to review Chapter 5 of *Biological Psychology*.

Answers to the labelling exercises can be found at the back of the book.

5.1 SINGLE VS DOUBLE DISSOCIATIONS

INTRODUCTION

The use of dissociations in experimental evidence is important for determining whether functions rely on different areas of the brain. However, it is only a double dissociation that allows the conclusion that two functions are separable within the brain.

───────────────── **COLOURING NOTES 5.1** ─────────────────

Panel A. For each image, colour:

☐ The screen in blue
☐ The computer (i.e. part that houses the processor) in red

Panel B. In this scenario, the power to the screen is turned off. Indicate the elements that are powered on by colouring them in using the colours indicated in (A) above.

Panel C. In this scenario, the power to the computer (processor) is turned off. Indicate the elements that are powered on by colouring them in using the colours indicated in (A).

Circle together:

(a) The two images that represent a double dissociation in green
(b) The two images that represent a single dissociation in yellow

───

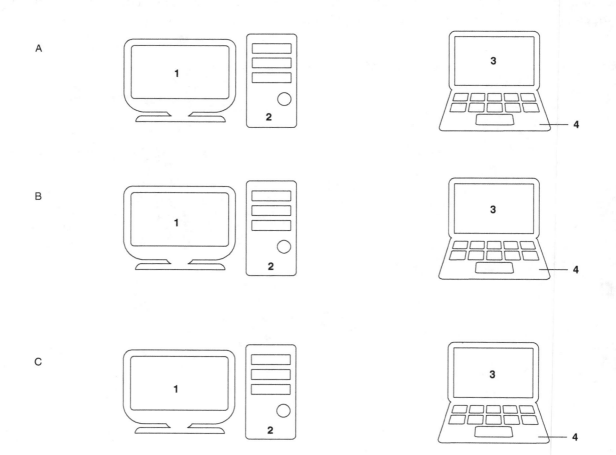

5.2 GRAPHICAL REPRESENTATION OF HOW MEMORY STRENGTH AND PREDICTION ERROR PROGRESS DURING LEARNING

INTRODUCTION

The Rescorla-Wagner rule of learning describes the amount that is learned on each learning as being related to (i) the amount that has already been learned [the existing memory strength] and (ii) the prediction error.

———————————————— **COLOURING NOTES 5.2** ————————————————

Draw lines on the graph as follows starting from the marker plotted on the graph:

☐ Orange for the memory strength at the start of each trial
☐ Red for the prediction error on each trial
☐ Blue for the amount learned on each trial

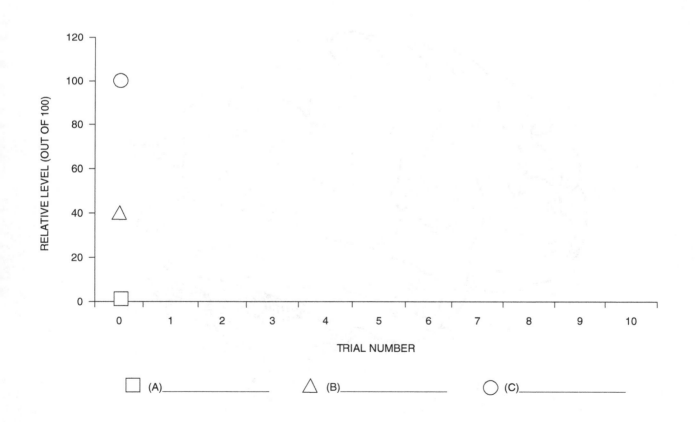

5.3 PROGRESSION OF MEMORY-RELATED PROPERTIES IN THE VENTRAL VISUAL PATHWAY

INTRODUCTION

Neurons in the ventral visual pathway of the brain differ in their memory-related (mnemonic) properties. In some areas, the neurons are active only when a visual stimulus is present (perceptual neurons). In other areas, the neurons continue responding, even after the visual stimulus disappears, showing memory for the recent presentation (mnemonic neurons).

--- **COLOURING NOTES 5.3** ---

Label and colour:

☐ The occipital lobe (green)
☐ The temporal lobe (blue)
☐ Label which areas have more mnemonic or more perceptual neurons
☐ Draw a red arrow to represent the development of more mnemonic properties through the ventral visual pathway

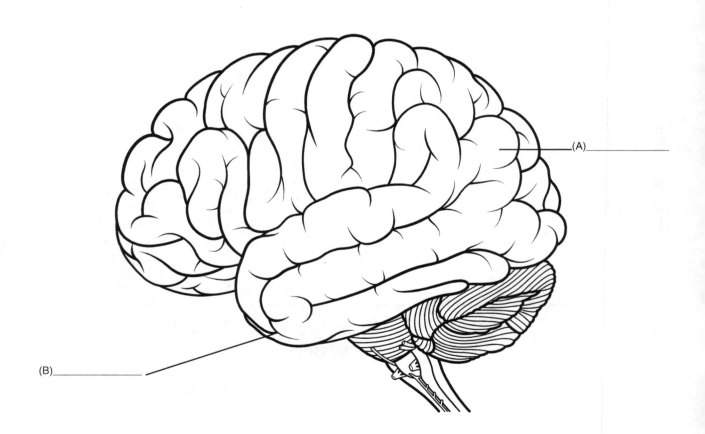

(A)_____

(B)_____

5.4 CONVERSION OF SHORT-TERM MEMORY INTO LONG-TERM MEMORY

INTRODUCTION

Recently acquired memories can exist in short-term and long-term forms, both of which can support memory expression. Short-term memory (STM) and long-term memory (LTM) differ in their dependence on the synthesis of new proteins.

─────────────── **COLOURING NOTES 5.4** ───────────────

Draw and label lines that represent STM and LTM ability to support memory expression:

☐ STM in red
☐ LTM in blue

Colour the areas of the graph that show when memory expression is supported by:

☐ STM in yellow
☐ LTM in orange

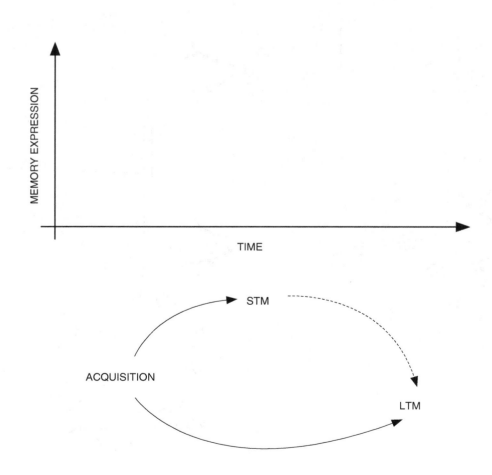

5.5 ASSOCIATIVE LTP

INTRODUCTION

Long-term potentiation can exist in non-associative and associative forms. Associative LTP involves two input pathways being active at the same time; one strong and one weaker.

--- **COLOURING NOTES 5.5** ---

Label:

☐ The output neuron
☐ The input neurons

Colour:

☐ One of the input neurons in red to denote the strong input pathway
☐ One of the input neurons in blue to denote the weaker input pathway
☐ The output neuron in green

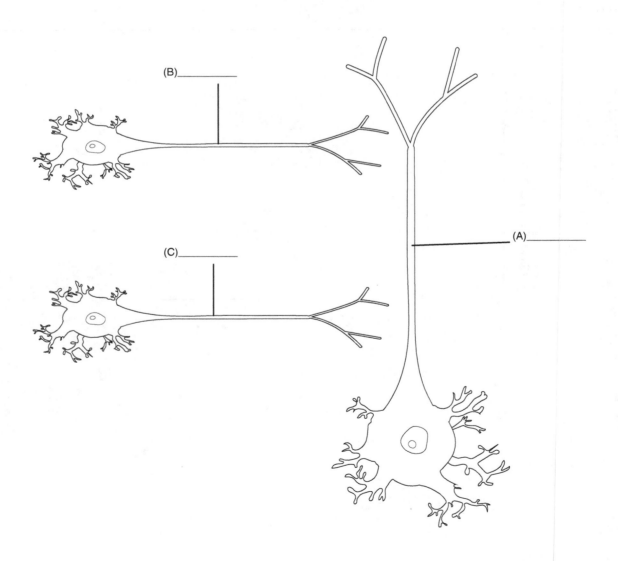

5.6 INCREASING OUTPUT VIA LTP

INTRODUCTION

LTP increases the strength of a synapse. This intuitively can lead to the increase of the output of a network in response to the same input.

In this schematic, the output neuron is on the right (A), with the main input neuron bottom left (B). The top left neuron is an inhibitory interneuron (C).

———————— COLOURING NOTES 5.6 ————————

Identify, label and colour:

☐   The output neuron (blue)
☐   The input neuronal cell body (yellow)
☐   The interneuron (pink)

☐   Draw the axonal projection from the input neuron to the output neuron (yellow line)
☐   You can draw in the projections to and from the interneuron as well, if you like (yellow)
☐   Colour excitatory synapses in green
☐   Colour inhibitory synapse in red
☐   Label the synapse(s) that are strengthened by LTP to increase activity in the output neuron

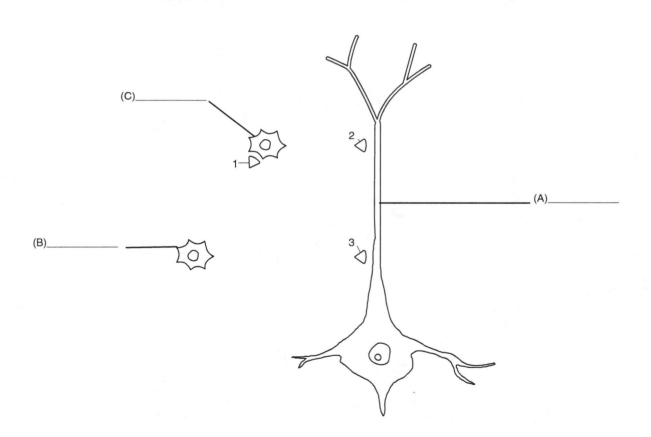

5.7 INCREASING OUTPUT VIA LTD

INTRODUCTION

LTD decreases the strength of a synapse. This can, rather counterintuitively, also lead to the increase of the output of a network in response to the same input. Again, in this schematic, the output neuron is on the right, with the main input neuron bottom left. The top left neuron is an interneuron.

COLOURING NOTES 5.7

Label and colour:

☐ The output neuron (blue)
☐ The input neuronal cell body (yellow)
☐ The interneuron (pink)

Draw:

☐ The axonal projection from the input neuron to the output neuron in yellow
☐ The axonal projection from the input neuron to the interneuron in yellow
☐ The axonal projection from the interneuron to the output neuron in orange

Colour:

☐ Excitatory synapses in green
☐ Inhibitory synapses in red

Label:

☐ The synapse(s) that are weakened by LTD to increase activity in the output neuron
☐ Any neurons whose activity is reduced at the same time as the ouput neuron being more active

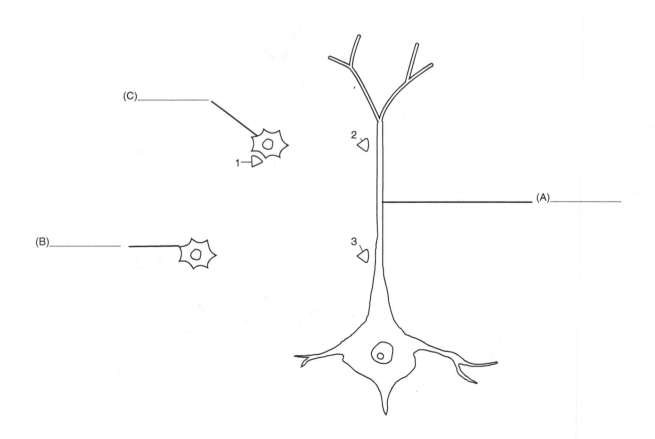

5.8 THE HIPPOCAMPUS

INTRODUCTION

The hippocampus is often the area of the brain most readily associated with memory, particularly episodic memory and spatial memory. Hippocampal damage not only impairs the acquisition of new spatial/episodic memories, but also impairs some previously acquired memories. HM was a famous neuropsychological patient who had his entire medial temporal lobe (which includes the hippocampus) removed on both sides of the brain, resulting in an inability to form new conscious memories.

─────────────────── **COLOURING NOTES 5.8** ───────────────────

☐   Identify and colour the hippocampus orange

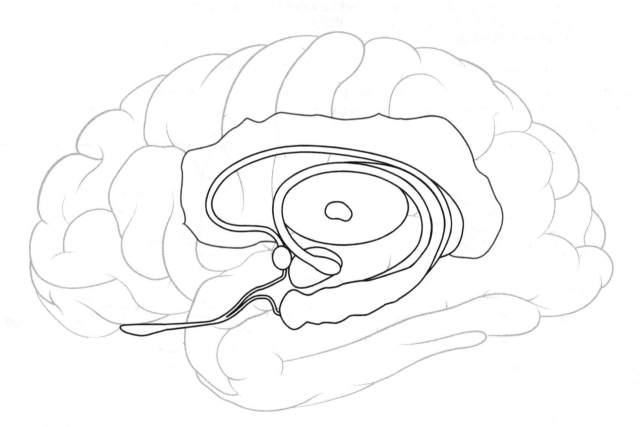

Adapted from original creation by Hrejsa/Body Scientific Intl. for SAGE Publishing

5.9 SYSTEMS CONSOLIDATION

INTRODUCTION

Systems consolidation seeks to explain the observation that damage to the hippocampus impairs recent episodic memories more than older remote memories. The explanation for this temporally graded retrograde amnesia centres upon the different rates of learning in the hippocampus and cortex.

COLOURING NOTES 5.9

Panel A. This shows the network at baseline, before learning. Colour:

☐ Cortical units in yellow
☐ Hippocampal units in blue

Panel B. This shows the network soon after learning.

☐ Draw/colour red lines between units to show the plasticity that underpins the memory
☐ Colour the units that are integral to the memory in orange
☐ Colour the remaining units as in (A)

Panel C. This shows the network long after learning (i.e. after systems consolidation is complete).

☐ Draw/colour green lines between units to show the plasticity that underpins the memory
☐ Colour the units that are integral to the memory in purple
☐ Colour the remaining units as in (A)

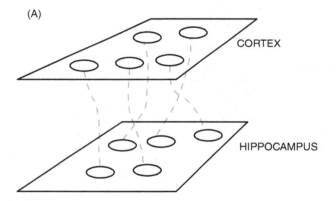

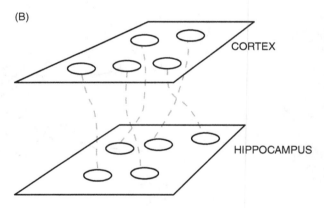

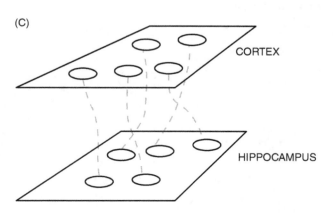

5.10 MULTIPLE TRACE THEORY

INTRODUCTION

Multiple trace theory suggests that episodic memories always rely upon the hippocampus for their retrieval. However, it is argued that this theory can still account for temporally-graded retrograde amnesia, while also explaining the occurrence of 'flat' gradients of retrograde amnesia.

COLOURING NOTES 5.10

Panel A. This shows the network at baseline, before learning.

Colour:

☐ Cortical units in yellow
☐ Hippocampal units in blue

Panel B. This shows the network soon after learning.

☐ Draw/colour red lines between units to show the plasticity that underpins the memory
☐ Colour the units that are integral to the memory in orange
☐ Colour the remaining units as in (A)

Panel C. This shows the network long after learning (i.e. after multiple rounds of retrieval).

☐ Draw/colour green lines between units to show the plasticity that underpins the memory
☐ Colour the units that are integral to the memory in purple
☐ Colour the remaining units as in (A)

Panel D. This shows the effect of a partial hippocampal lesion long after learning.

☐ Colour one hippocampal unit in black
☐ Draw/colour green lines between the remaining units replicating what you have done in (C)
☐ Colour the units that are integral to the preserved memory in purple

(A)

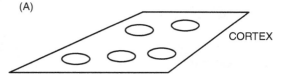
CORTEX

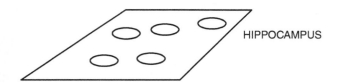
HIPPOCAMPUS

(B)

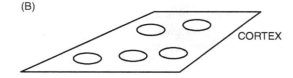
CORTEX

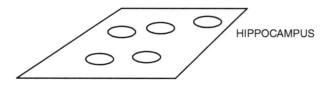
HIPPOCAMPUS

(C)

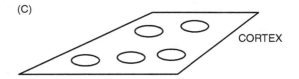
CORTEX

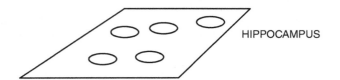
HIPPOCAMPUS

(D)

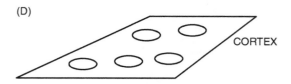
CORTEX

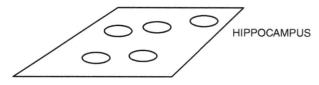
HIPPOCAMPUS

5.11 NEURAL CIRCUITRY OF MEMORY EXTINCTION

INTRODUCTION

Memory extinction involves the inhibition of the originally learned memory, and is not unlearning. Importantly, the extinction memory is more linked to the context of extinction learning than is the original learning to its context. This gives rise to the phenomenon of 'renewal', in which the original memory recovers when tested outside the extinction context.

COLOURING NOTES 5.11

Before extinction:

- ☐ Label each circle with the appropriate anatomical area
- ☐ Colour the CS in red
- ☐ Colour the infralimbic cortex in yellow
- ☐ Colour the amygdala in orange
- ☐ Colour the hippocampus in green
- ☐ Draw blue arrow(s) to show which brain areas are activated by the CS
- ☐ Draw an arrow by 'Fear response' to show whether the response is activated or inhibited

After extinction – in the extinction context:

- ☐ Label and colour the image as above
- ☐ Draw blue arrow(s) to show which brain areas are activated by the CS
- ☐ Draw an arrow by 'Fear response' to show whether the response is activated or inhibited
- ☐ Draw and label relevant lines between the brain areas to show how the fear response is modulated

After extinction – in a different context:

- ☐ Label and colour the image as above
- ☐ Draw blue arrow(s) to show which brain areas are activated by the CS
- ☐ Draw an arrow by 'Fear response' to show whether the response is activated or inhibited
- ☐ Draw and label relevant lines between the brain areas to show how the fear response is modulated

---

BEFORE EXTINCTION

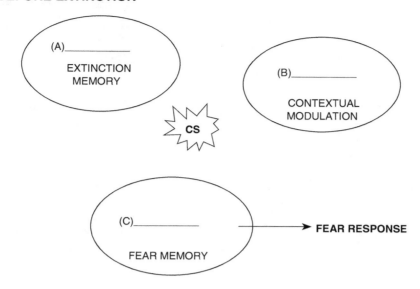

(A)_____
EXTINCTION
MEMORY

(B)_____
CONTEXTUAL
MODULATION

CS

(C)_____
FEAR MEMORY

→ **FEAR RESPONSE**

AFTER EXTINCTION – IN THE EXTINCTION CONTEXT

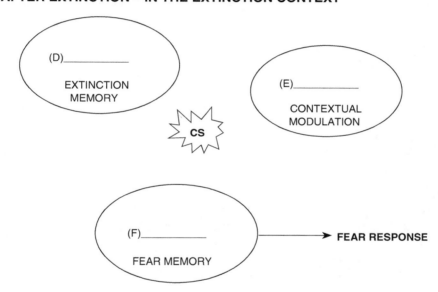

(D)_____
EXTINCTION
MEMORY

(E)_____
CONTEXTUAL
MODULATION

CS

(F)_____
FEAR MEMORY

→ **FEAR RESPONSE**

AFTER EXTINCTION – IN A DIFFERENT CONTEXT

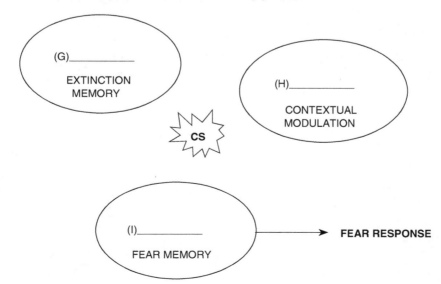

(G)_____
EXTINCTION
MEMORY

(H)_____
CONTEXTUAL
MODULATION

CS

(I)_____
FEAR MEMORY

→ **FEAR RESPONSE**

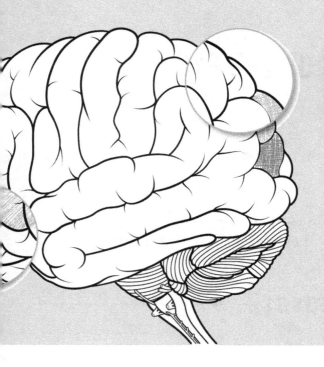

CHAPTER 6

SENSORY SYSTEMS

INTRODUCTION

Our sensory systems provide us with descriptions of the world that can reliably guide our behaviour. Each of our senses is equipped with specialised receptor cells that respond to a particular physical aspect of the environment. For example, in vision, photoreceptors respond to light; in hearing, balance, touch and proprioception, mechanoreceptors respond to physical distortion of the receptor cell; and in taste and smell, chemoreceptors respond in the presence of particular molecules. Each different pattern of physical stimulation produces a different pattern of response across the relevant receptors. And, in each sensory modality, this pattern of response is conveyed to specialised regions of the brain. This chapter will help you understand the components of sensory systems. Remember to review Chapter 6 of *Biological Psychology*.

Answers to the labelling exercises can be found at the back of the book.

6.1 COMPONENTS OF THE EYE

INTRODUCTION

The eye is a sphere about 2.5 cm in diameter and five sixths of it is concealed within the orbit, with one sixth visible. It has three principal components:

1 The three-layered wall
2 The optical components that focus light and regulate its entry to the eye
3 Neurological components that convert light to electrochemical energy to generate images

---
COLOURING NOTES 6.1

Colour and label the following:

- ☐ Cornea (blue)
- ☐ Iris (purple)
- ☐ Lens
- ☐ Optic nerve (red)
- ☐ Pupil
- ☐ Retina (orange)

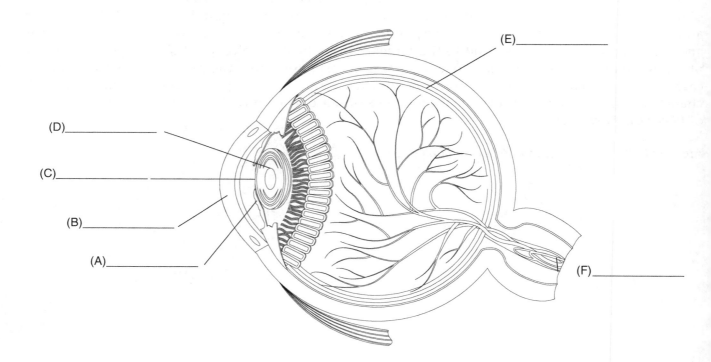

6.2 THE EYE CAPTURES LIGHT

INTRODUCTION

The first step in seeing is to measure the amount of light at each point in the image. The eye captures some of the light that is reflected from surfaces and objects and forms it into an image. This process takes place in the retina.

COLOURING NOTES 6.2 ———

Label:

- ☐ Cornea
- ☐ Iris
- ☐ Light
- ☐ Fixation point
- ☐ Lens
- ☐ Retina
- ☐ Pupil
- ☐ Optic nerve
- ☐ In black, colour in the three lines from the fixation point though the lens onto the retina

---

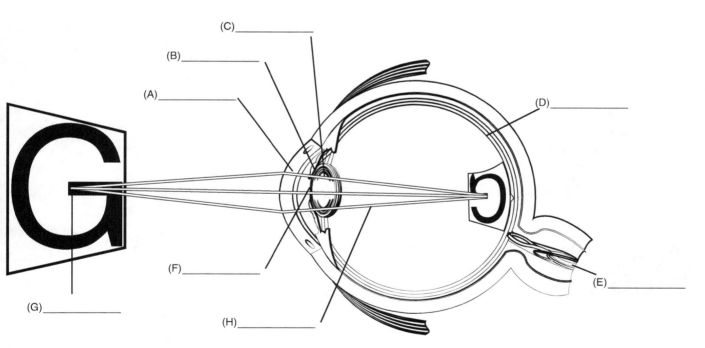

Adapted from Garrett, *Brain and Behavior* (2020). Sage; and Figure 26-1 in Kandel, E.R., Schwartz, J.H., Jessell, T.M, Siegelbaum, S.A., Hudspeth, A.J. and Mack, S. (2012). *Principles of Neural Science*, 5th edition. McGraw Hill Education.

6.3 THE RETINA

INTRODUCTION

The retina consists of a network of receptors, interneurons, ganglion cells and blood vessels. Light has to pass through these layers before it reaches the photoreceptors (rods and cones), which respond to light.

--- **COLOURING NOTES 6.3** ---

Colour and label:

- ☐ Amacrine cell (red)
- ☐ Bipolar cell (blue)
- ☐ Cone (green)
- ☐ Ganglion cell (orange)
- ☐ Rod (purple)

Label:

- ☐ Cornea
- ☐ Fovea
- ☐ Horizontal cell
- ☐ Iris
- ☐ Lens
- ☐ Macula
- ☐ Optic nerve
- ☐ Pupil
- ☐ Retina
- ☐ Vitreous gel

(D)_____

(E)_____

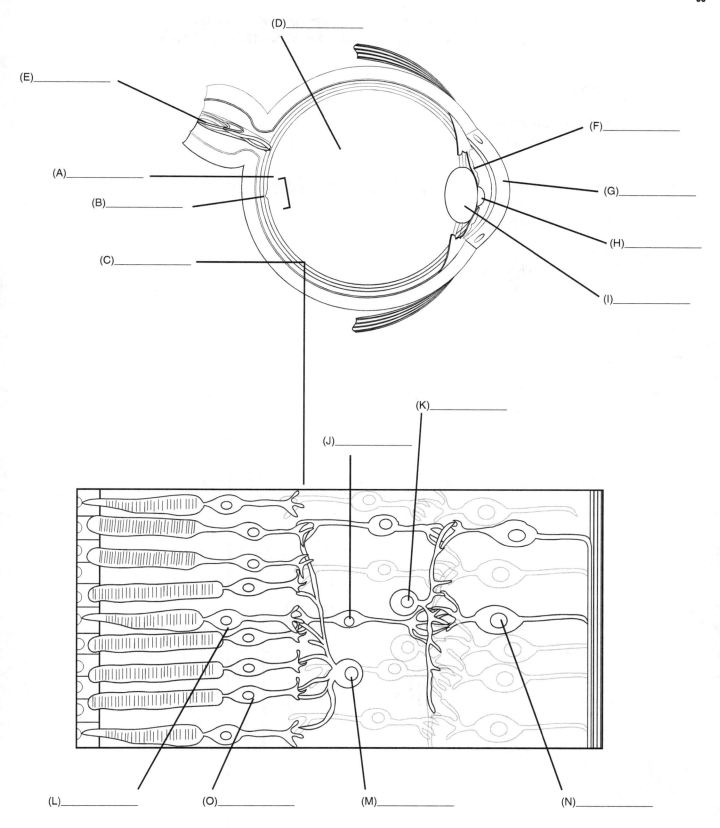

(A)_____

(B)_____

(C)_____

(F)_____

(G)_____

(H)_____

(I)_____

(K)_____

(J)_____

(L)_____

(O)_____

(M)_____

(N)_____

6.4 CONE AND ROD RECEPTORS

INTRODUCTION

Both rods and cones are composed of synaptic terminals, inner segments that contain the cell bodies and outer segments of membranous discs that contain photo pigments.

--- **COLOURING NOTES 6.4** ---

Colour and label the following:

☐ Rod photoreceptors (red)
☐ Cone photoreceptors (blue)

Label:

☐ Synaptic terminals
☐ Inner segments
☐ Cell bodies
☐ Outer segments
☐ Membranous discs containing photo pigments

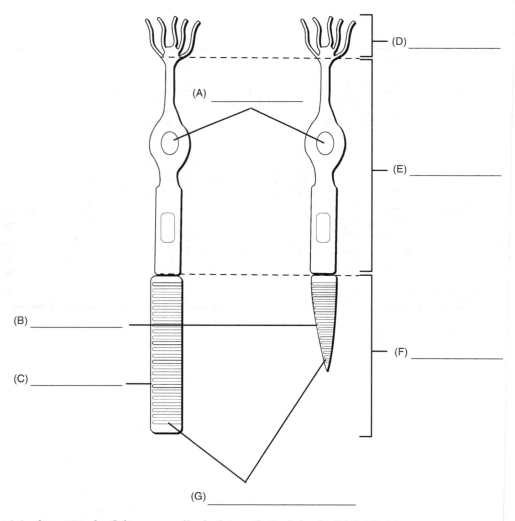

Adapted from original creation by Scheuerman/Body Scientific Intl. for SAGE Publishing

6.5 RETINAL GANGLION RECEPTIVE FIELDS

INTRODUCTION

Ganglion cells are the output stage of the retina. The axons of retinal ganglion cells form the optic nerve. Each retinal ganglion cell responds to light in a small region of the retina, called the cell's receptive field. Ganglion cell receptive fields are typically circular and consist of two distinct subregions – one exciting the cell, the other inhibiting it, as shown below. This 'centre–surround' arrangement ensures that retinal ganglion cells do not respond to the uniform regions that make up much of the image, so that the neural image provided by the photoreceptors is reduced to a kind of 'neural line-drawing' at the retinal ganglion cells, which carry the output from the retina. The + and – symbols represent each subregion's response to light. In a + 'on' subregion, light increases the ganglion cell's response while darkness decreases it. In a – 'off' subregion, the reverse is true. There are roughly equal numbers of on-centre and off-centre cells.

COLOURING NOTES 6.5

☐   Label the on responses and off responses of the receptive fields
☐   Colour the centre blue and the surround pink

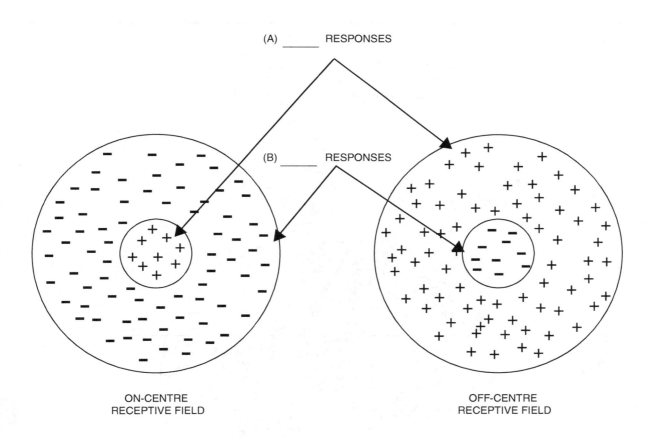

(A) _____ RESPONSES

(B) _____ RESPONSES

ON-CENTRE
RECEPTIVE FIELD

OFF-CENTRE
RECEPTIVE FIELD

6.6 THE VISUAL PATHWAY

INTRODUCTION

The optic nerve projects to the optic chiasma, where half the fibres from each retina cross over in an arrangement that ensures that the two images of an object – one in each eye – are processed in the same place; objects to our left project to the right hemisphere, and vice versa.

COLOURING NOTES 6.6

Label:

- ☐ Lateral geniculate nucleus
- ☐ Left visual field
- ☐ Nasal
- ☐ Optic chiasma
- ☐ Optic radiation
- ☐ Primary visual cortex
- ☐ Right visual field
- ☐ Superior colliculus
- ☐ Temporal
- ☐ Colour the connection from the temporal half of the retina green and the connection from the nasal half of the retina red

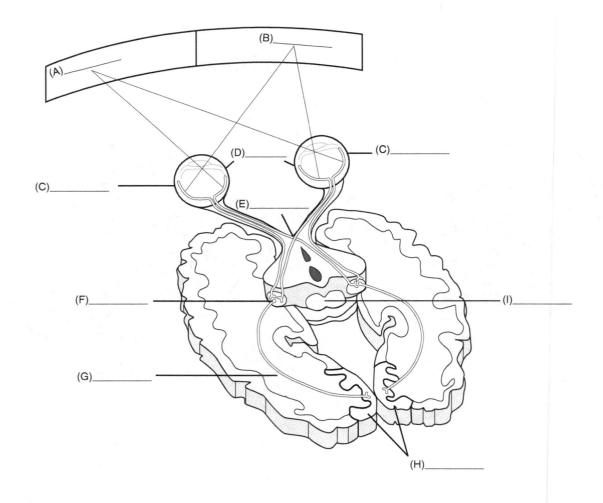

6.7 THE VENTRAL AND DORSAL VISUAL PATHWAYS

INTRODUCTION

Visual perception includes ventral and dorsal stream processes. The 'what' stream originating in the parvocellular layers of the lateral geniculate nucleus projects ventrally to the temporal and inferotemporal cortex, whereas the magnocellular 'where' stream projects dorsally to the parietal cortex.

COLOURING NOTES 6.7

Label:

☐ Inferotemporal cortex
☐ Parietal cortex

Colour and label:

☐ Dorsal stream (blue)
☐ Ventral stream (pink)

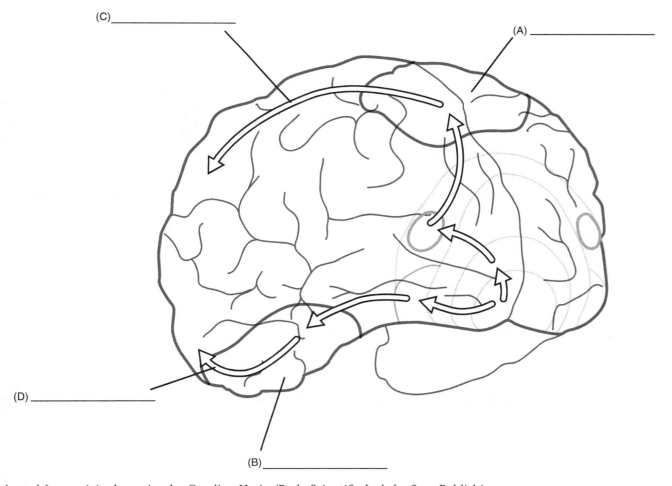

(C)_____

(A) _____

(D) _____

(B) _____

Adapted from original creation by Carolina Hrejsa/Body Scientific Intl. for Sage Publishing.

6.8 THE AUDITORY SYSTEM

INTRODUCTION

Sounds are caused by movements in the external world creating waves of pressure variation in the air that are picked up by the tympanic membrane, or ear drum, in each of our ears. Periodic stimuli cause the ear drum to vibrate at the same frequency as the stimulus and these vibrations are transmitted by tiny bones, or ossicles, in the middle ear to the oval window of the cochlea.

—— COLOURING NOTES 6.8 ——

Label:

- ☐ Anvil
- ☐ Auditory nerve
- ☐ Cochlea
- ☐ Ear canal
- ☐ Ear drum
- ☐ Eustachian tube

- ☐ Hammer
- ☐ Inner ear
- ☐ Middle ear
- ☐ Outer ear
- ☐ Pinna
- ☐ Stirrup

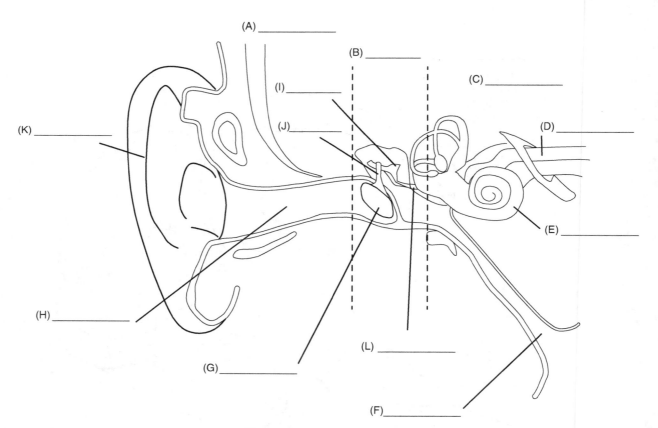

Adapted from Barnes, J. (2013). *Essential Biological Psychology*. London: Sage.

6.9 THE COCHLEA

INTRODUCTION

Each pulse of the oval window causes a pulse to travel along the basilar membrane of the cochlea. Each point on the basilar membrane moves up and down as the pulse travels past it and this mechanically distorts the cilia of the inner hair cells that are arrayed along the membrane and act as the auditory receptors. The distortion causes graded receptor potentials in the inner hair cells which in turn cause action potentials in the fibres of the auditory nerve innervating the basilar membrane.

––––––––––––––––––––––––––––––– **COLOURING NOTES 6.9** –––––––––––––––––––––––––––––––

Colour and label (note, one label appears twice):

- ☐ Inner hair cells (red)
- ☐ Outer hair cells (red)
- ☐ Basilar membrane (grey)

Label:

- ☐ Auditory nerve
- ☐ Tectorial membrane

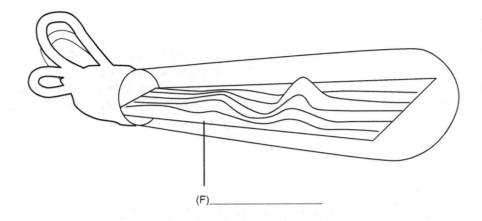

(F)_____

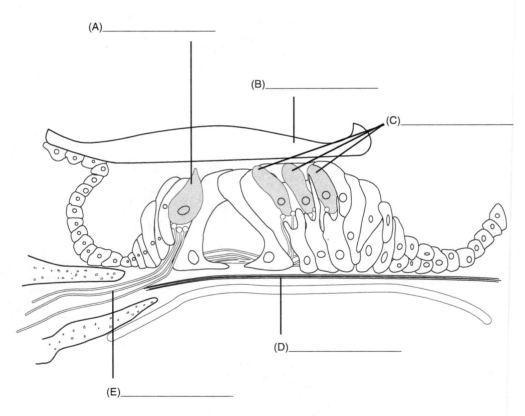

(A)_____

(B)_____

(C)_____

(D)_____

(E)_____

Adapted from Barnes, J. (2013). *Essential Biological Psychology*. London: Sage.

6.10 DIAGRAM OF THE AUDITORY PATHWAY

INTRODUCTION

The first stage in the auditory pathway receiving input from both ears is the superior olivary complex. Leaving this relay, a third neuron carries information up to the inferior colliculus. A last relay, before the cortex, occurs in the medial geniculate body. The final neuron of the primary auditory pathway links the medial geniculate body to the auditory cortex.

———————————— COLOURING NOTES 6.10 ————————————

Label:

☐ Cochlea
☐ Superior olivary nucleus
☐ Medial geniculate body
☐ Inferior colliculus
☐ Primary auditory cortex (A1)
☐ Auditory nerve

Colour:

☐ Cochlea (yellow)
☐ The link between the cochlea and the superior olivary nucleus (red)
☐ The link between the superior olivary nucleus and the inferior colliculus (blue)
☐ The link between the inferior colliculus and the medial geniculate nucleus (green)
☐ The link between the medial geniculate nucleus and A1 (purple)

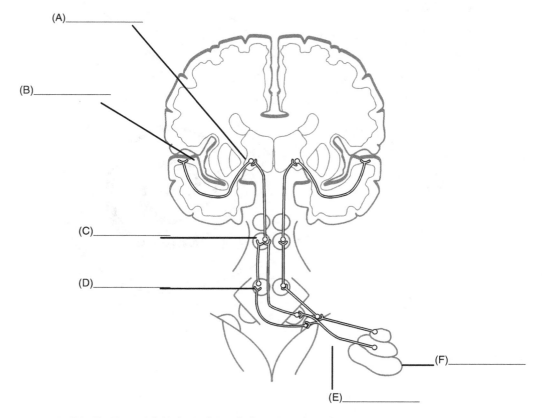

Adapted from Barnes, J. (2013). *Essential Biological Psychology*. London: Sage.

6.11 THE VESTIBULAR SYSTEM

INTRODUCTION

The vestibular system is primarily concerned with maintaining balance by detecting movements of the head. It consists of three semicircular canals and two small organs, the utricle and saccule, that, together with the cochlea, form the inner ear.

──────── COLOURING NOTES 6.11 ────────

Label:

☐ Semicircular canals
☐ Utricle
☐ Saccule
☐ Cochlea

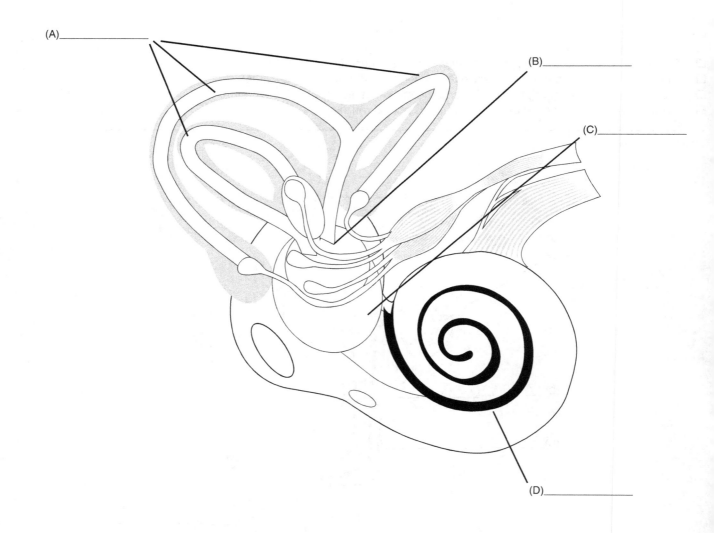

6.12 THE UTRICLE AND SACCULE

INTRODUCTION

In the utricle and saccule, hair cells project into a gelatinous membrane incorporating small, relatively heavy calcium carbonate crystals (otoliths). These hair cells signal linear acceleration; the heavy gelatinous membrane lags behind during acceleration and overshoots during deceleration, distorting the hair cells and causing a graded response of the appropriate polarity. The cilia in the utricle and saccule are arranged in different directions so that, between them, they detect movement in any direction.

──────────── COLOURING NOTES 6.12 ────────────

Colour and label the following:

☐ Otoliths (purple)
☐ Hair cells (blue)
☐ Gelatinous membrane (pink)
☐ Neurons (yellow)

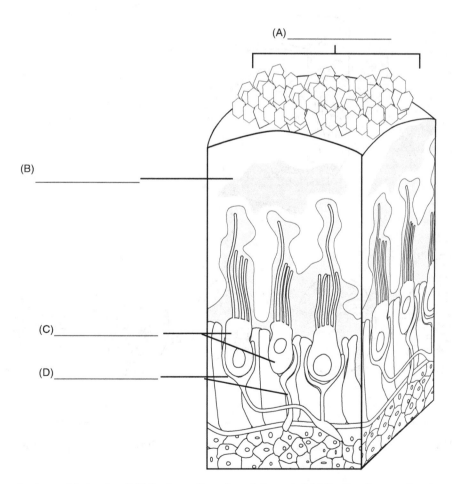

Adapted from Garrett, *Brain and Behavior* (2020). Sage. Based on Martini (1988). *Fundamentals of Anatomy and Physiology*, fourth edition. Upper Saddle River, NJ: Prentice Hall.

6.13 THE MAIN TYPES OF TOUCH RECEPTOR IN THE SKIN

INTRODUCTION

Touch receptors are modified ends of myelinated sensory nerves. They are specialised to detect different aspects of the stimulus, such as pressure or stretching of the skin, by different mechanical structures surrounding the nerve ending. In addition to unmodified nerve endings, there are four distinct types of touch receptor: Merkel's discs, Meissner's corpuscles, Ruffini endings and Pacinian corpuscles.

COLOURING NOTES 6.13

Colour and label the following:

- ☐ Free nerve endings (purple)
- ☐ Hair (brown)
- ☐ Merkel's disc (black)

- ☐ Meissner's corpuscle (blue)
- ☐ Ruffini endings (pink)
- ☐ Pacinian corpuscle (green)

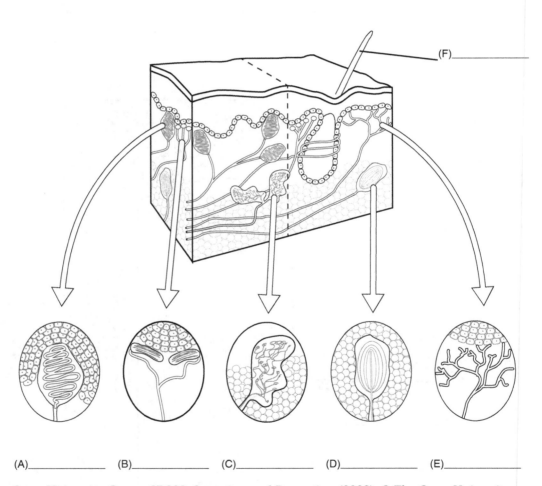

(F)_____

(A)_____ (B)_____ (C)_____ (D)_____ (E)_____

Adapted from Open University Course SD329: Sensation and Perception (2003). © The Open University.

6.14 THE DORSAL COLUMN–MEDIAL LEMNISCAL (DCML) PATHWAY

INTRODUCTION

The dorsal column-medial lemniscal (DCML) pathway deals with touch sensations from the body. Touch-sensitive fibres enter the spinal cord and ascend directly in the dorsal columns through the medulla. Medullary neurons cross the midline and project in the medial lemniscus to the ventral posterior nucleus (VPN) of the thalamus. VPN cells project to the primary somatosensory cortex (S1) on the post-central gyrus. S1 projects to many sensory and motor cortical areas.

──────────────── **COLOURING NOTES 6.14** ────────────────

Label the following (note that one label appears twice):

- ☐ Spinal cord
- ☐ Medulla
- ☐ Pons
- ☐ Midbrain
- ☐ Cerebral cortex
- ☐ Primary somatosensory cortex (S1)
- ☐ Dorsal root ganglion cells
- ☐ Dorsal column nuclei
- ☐ Medial lemniscus
- ☐ Ventral posterior nucleus

RIGHT   LEFT

(K)_____

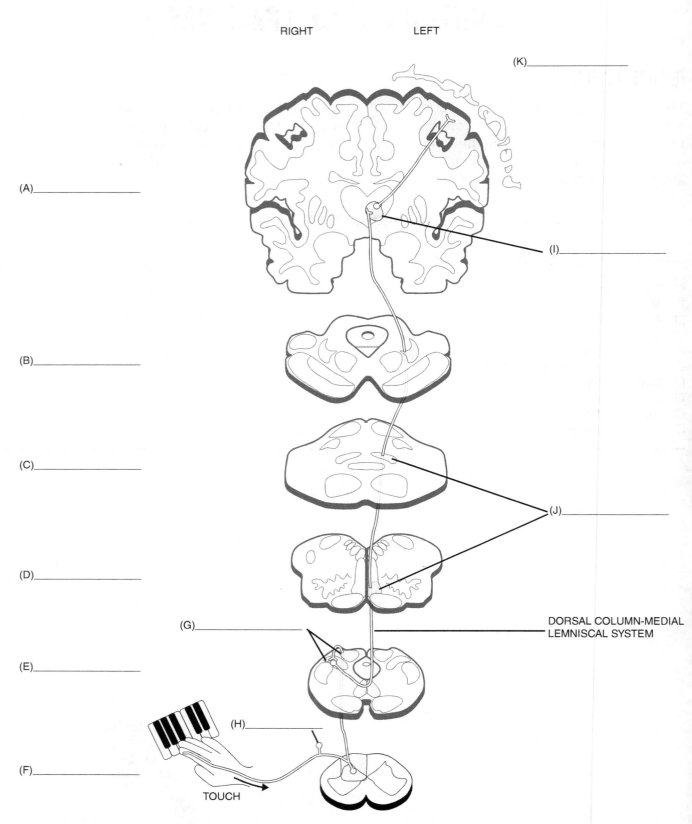

(A)_____

(I)_____

(B)_____

(C)_____

(J)_____

(D)_____

DORSAL COLUMN-MEDIAL
LEMNISCAL SYSTEM

(G)_____

(E)_____

(H)_____

(F)_____

TOUCH

Adapted from MacKinnon, C.D. (2018). 'Chapter 1: Sensorimotor anatomy of gait, balance, and falls', *Handbook of Clinical Neurology*, Vol 159: 3–26. © Elsevier. Used with permission.

6.15 THE DESCENDING PAIN INHIBITION CIRCUIT

INTRODUCTION

Fibres concerned with pain project downwards from the prefrontal cortex and hypothalamus, via the periaqueductal grey (PAG) in the midbrain, to 'gates' in the spinal cord. This tract makes use of endogenous opioids, which are neuromodulators acting upon specific opioid receptors, and which are known to be involved in pain relief.

COLOURING NOTES 6.15

Label:

☐ Periaqueductal grey area
☐ Midbrain
☐ Pons
☐ Medulla
☐ Spinal cord
☐ Endogenous opioids

Colour:

☐ The descending pathway (blue)
☐ The ascending pathway (red)

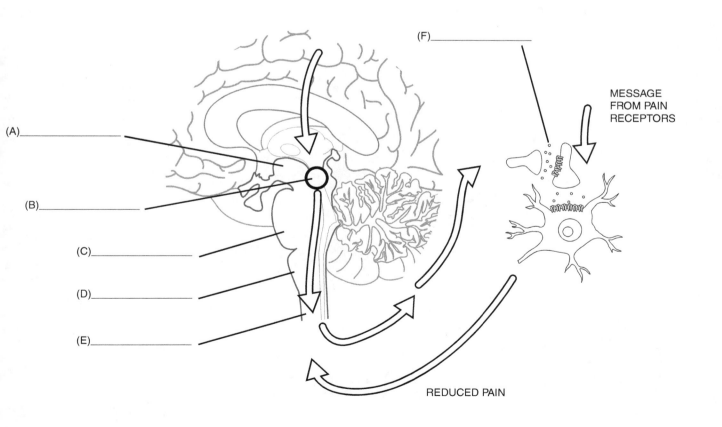

(F)_____

MESSAGE
FROM PAIN
RECEPTORS

(A)_____

(B)_____

(C)_____

(D)_____

(E)_____

REDUCED PAIN

6.16 TASTE PATHWAY FROM TONGUE TO BRAIN

INTRODUCTION

On the tongue, receptor cells are clustered together in taste buds. The receptors project in three different cranial nerves (the chorda tympani – which is a branch of the facial nerve, the glossopharyngeal nerve, and the vagus nerve) via the nucleus of the solitary tract to the ventral posterior medial nucleus of the thalamus, thence to the primary gustatory cortex, which is part of the insular cortex.

—————————————— **COLOURING NOTES 6.16** ——————————————

Colour and label the following:

- ☐ Taste receptor cell (brown)
- ☐ Tongue (pink)
- ☐ Facial nerve (purple)
- ☐ Glossopharyngeal nerve (blue)
- ☐ Vagus nerve (red)
- ☐ Nucleus of the solitary tract (green)
- ☐ Ventral posterior medial thalamic nucleus (yellow)
- ☐ Primary gustatory cortex (orange)

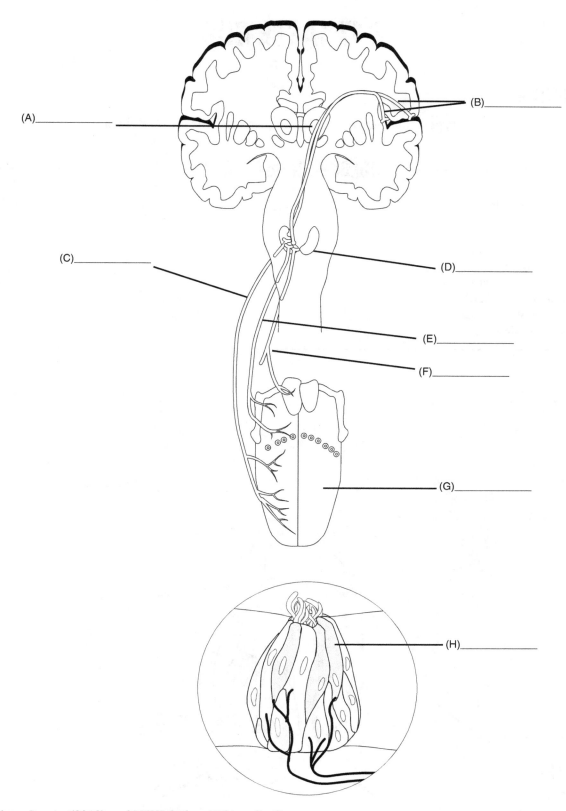

(A)_____

(B)_____

(C)_____

(D)_____

(E)_____

(F)_____

(G)_____

(H)_____

Adapted from Barnes (2013) and NEUROtiker, Wikimedia Commons.

6.17 TASTE BUD

INTRODUCTION

Taste buds consist of three types of cells: taste cells, supporting cells and basal cells.

COLOURING NOTES 6.17

Colour and label the following:

- ☐ Taste pore
- ☐ Gustatory hair (light blue)
- ☐ Gustatory receptor cells (dark blue)
- ☐ Supporting cells (green)
- ☐ Sensory neurons (yellow)
- ☐ Connective tissue
- ☐ Basal cells (purple)

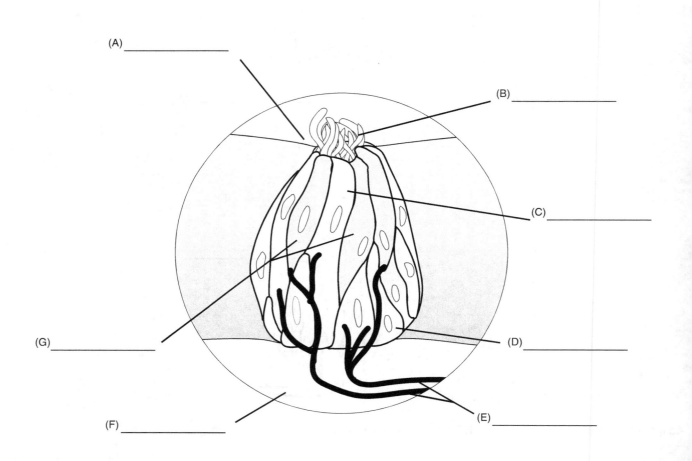

(A) _____

(B) _____

(C) _____

(D) _____

(E) _____

(F) _____

(G) _____

6.18 OLFACTION

INTRODUCTION

Olfaction, or smell, is the second chemical sense with the primary sense organ in the olfactory mucosa in the superior nasal cavity. Olfaction is highly sensitive, with some people able to identify up to 10,000 smells using the 10–20 million olfactory cells in the olfactory mucosa. Supporting cells provide electrical insulation, protection and nourishment to the olfactory neurons while also detoxifying chemicals, while the basal cells divide and differentiate into new olfactory neurons.

COLOURING NOTES 6.18

Label:

☐ Olfactory neuron
☐ Dendrite
☐ Cilia
☐ Olfactory vesicle
☐ Olfactory bulb
☐ Cribriform formina
☐ Axon

Colour and label:

☐ Basal cells (purple)
☐ Supporting cells (blue)

Colour:

☐ The olfactory tract and axons (green)

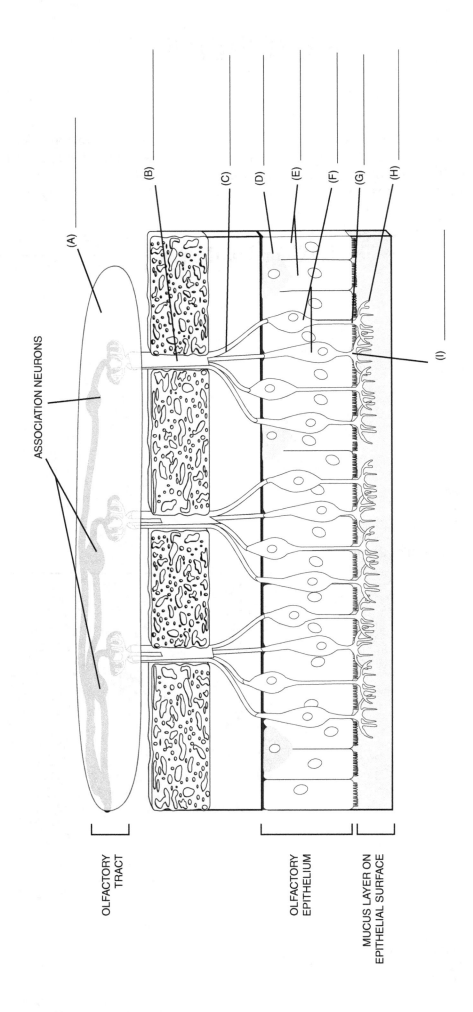

(A)

(B)

(C)

(D)

(E)

(F)

(G)

(H)

(I)

ASSOCIATION NEURONS

OLFACTORY
TRACT

OLFACTORY
EPITHELIUM

MUCUS LAYER ON
EPITHELIAL SURFACE

6.19 THE MAIN OLFACTORY PATHWAY

INTRODUCTION

Olfactory neurons project in the olfactory nerve to the olfactory bulb where they synapse with mitral cells in distinct spherical structures called glomeruli (singular = glomerulus). Many olfactory neurons project to just a few mitral cells. Unlike other senses, mitral cells project directly to the piriform cortex (the primary olfactory cortex) without a synapse in the thalamus. Mitral cells also project directly to the amygdala and entorhinal cortex. From the piriform cortex, smell information passes to the orbitofrontal cortex, where it is integrated with taste and visual information.

COLOURING NOTES 6.19

Colour and label the following:

☐ Olfactory neurons (blue)
☐ Glomerulus (yellow)
☐ Mitral cells (pink)

☐ Piriform cortex (the primary olfactory cortex) (purple)
☐ Amygdala (green)
☐ Entorhinal cortex (red)

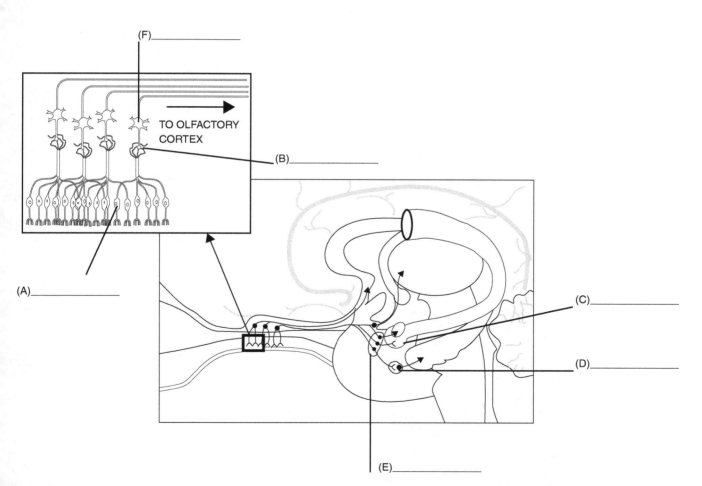

Adapted from The Open University Course SD329: Sensation and Perception (2003) © The Open University.

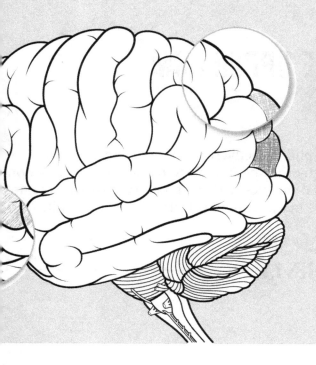

CHAPTER 7

MOTOR CONTROL

INTRODUCTION

Motor control occurs with a minimum of conscious awareness, yet even the simple act of reaching out and turning the page of this book involves many complex processes coordinated by the brain. Your basal ganglia select the appropriate movements and your posterior parietal cortex formulates a sophisticated plan specifying the sequence of movements required. This plan includes information about how and how hard to grasp the page, and relies upon knowledge gained through repeated trial and error by the cerebellum. The pre-motor cortex becomes active in anticipation of your movement, and your primary motor cortex responds to initiate the movement. The outputs from the motor cortex recruit the appropriate motor circuits in the spinal cord and set in train a series of events that cause muscles to contract and relax. Information from sensors in the muscles and joints is fed back to the cerebellum, which corrects any deviations from the plan and, if necessary, informs the parietal cortex of any changes needed for future plans. This chapter will help you understand these processes involved in motor control. Remember to review Chapter 7 of *Biological Psychology*.

Answers to the labelling exercises can be found at the back of the book.

7.1 MUSCLES OF THE UPPER ARM

INTRODUCTION

Muscles are attached to the skeleton by tendons and can pull, by actively shortening, but not push. Nor do they need to, for they are arranged in opposition to each other around joints so that active contraction of one muscle passively stretches the other. Often, several muscles work together as **agonists** and are opposed by several **antagonists**. For example, when the biceps contracts it flexes the arm, while contracting the triceps extends the arm.

COLOURING NOTES 7.1

Label:

☐ Biceps contracts
☐ Triceps relaxes
☐ Triceps contracts
☐ Biceps relaxes

Colour:

☐ The muscles (pink)
☐ The bones (brown)

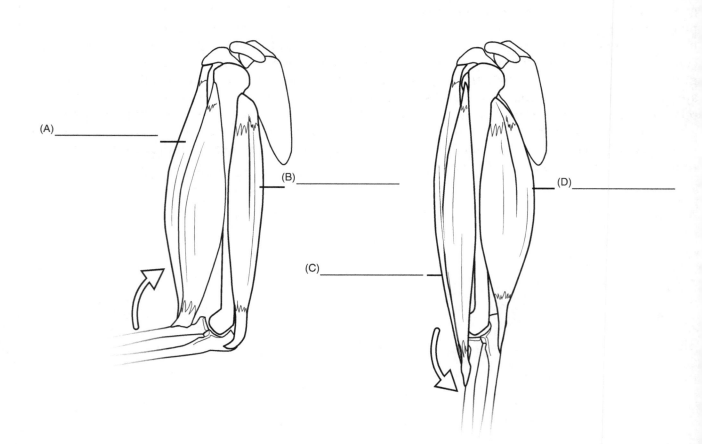

Adapted from Garrett, *Brain and Behavior* (2020). Sage; and Starr, C., and Taggart, R. (1989). *Biology: The Unity and Diversity of Life*. Pacific Grove, CA: Brooks/Cole.

7.2 THE NEUROMUSCULAR JUNCTION

INTRODUCTION

The arrival of a single action potential at a neuromuscular junction is sufficient to cause a brief contraction of the muscle fibre, called a twitch. Acetylcholine released at the junction causes an excitatory potential that opens voltage-gated Na+ channels in the muscle membrane and produces an action potential in the muscle fibre.

COLOURING NOTES 7.2

Colour and label the following:

- ☐ Muscle fibre (purple)
- ☐ Neuromuscular junction
- ☐ Axon of motor neuron (orange)
- ☐ Myofibrils (red)

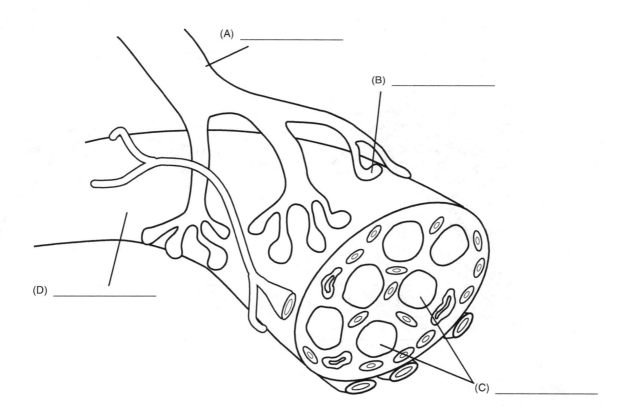

(A) _____

(B) _____

(D) _____

(C) _____

7.3 MUSCLE FIBRE CONTRACTION

INTRODUCTION

The release of Ca^{++} at the neuromuscular junction causes interleaved filaments of two proteins, actin and myosin, to slide over each other, shortening the muscle fibre. In the presence of Ca^{++}, the ends of individual myosin filaments form links that move like tiny oars, 'rowing' myosin along the actin. The filaments move in waves rather than all together, so that there are always some links between the actin and myosin. After the action potential, the Ca^{++} is mopped up, all the links are broken, and the muscle fibre relaxes.

COLOURING NOTES 7.3

Colour and label the following:

☐ Myosin filaments (brown)
☐ Actin filaments (yellow)

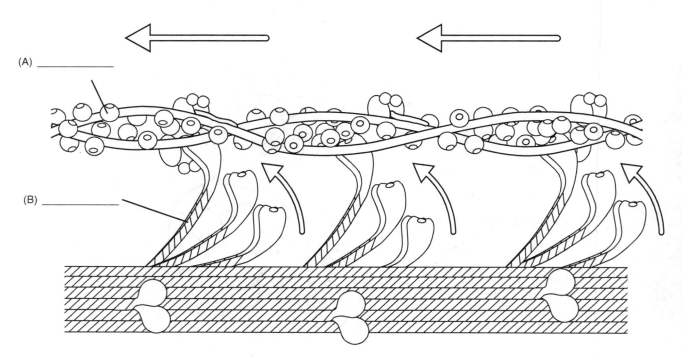

(A) _____

(B) _____

Adapted from Figure 10.7, *Principles of Anatomy and Physiology* (11th ed.), by Gerard J. Tortora and Bryan H. Derrickson, 2006, Hoboken, NJ: John Wiley & Sons

7.4 THE SPINAL STRETCH REFLEX

INTRODUCTION

The spinal stretch reflex is an example of the simplest system capable of producing an appropriate movement to an external stimulus. Muscle spindles, in parallel with the extrafusal fibres, detect stretching within a muscle and activate alpha motoneurons via a synapse in the spinal cord to produce a compensatory contraction according to a simple negative feedback system. Muscle spindles are wrapped around intrafusal muscle fibres, which are innervated by gamma motoneurons. Activity in a gamma motoneuron causes the intrafusal fibres to contract so that they maintain the same length as the extrafusal. Activity in spindles also inhibits the contraction of antagonistic muscles. This link provides the basis of a simple pathway through which to balance the tension in opposing muscles.

COLOURING NOTES 7.4

Label:

☐ Extrafusal fibre
☐ Spinal cord
☐ Intrafusal muscle fibres with spindle
☐ Antagonistic muscle
☐ Agonist muscle
☐ Sensory cell body

Colour:

☐ The alpha motoneuron loop (red)
☐ The gamma motoneuron pathway (green)
☐ The inhibitory loop to relax the antagonistic muscle (blue)

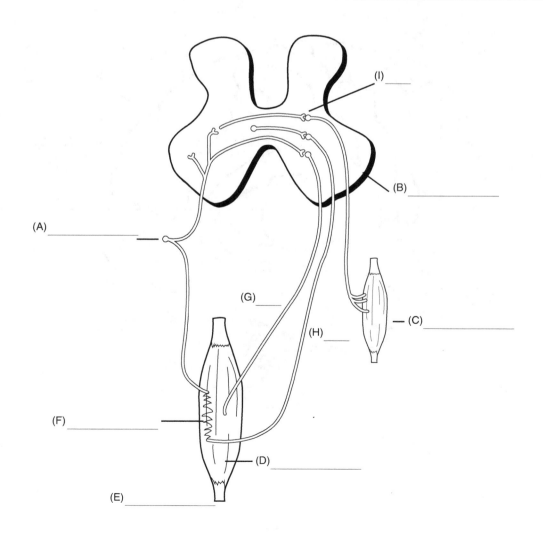

7.5 MAIN BRAIN AREAS INVOLVED IN MOTOR CONTROL

INTRODUCTION

Many brain regions are involved in motor control. The primary and secondary motor cortex form the final stages of central motor processing. They receive direct sensory input from the somatosensory and parietal cortex, involved in planning movements, and influence the motor circuits in the spinal cord. Through its direct pathways to the spinal cord, the motor cortex can initiate conscious movements. The motor cortex also has two indirect outputs forming loops through the basal ganglia, involved in the selection of appropriate movements, and through the cerebellum, involved in learning and refining complex sequences of actions.

―――――――――――――――――――― COLOURING NOTES 7.5 ――――――――――――

Colour and label the following:

☐ Primary motor cortex (red)
☐ Somatosensory cortex (yellow)
☐ Posterior parietal cortex (green)

☐ Basal ganglia (orange)
☐ Cerebellum (grey)
☐ Secondary motor cortex (blue)

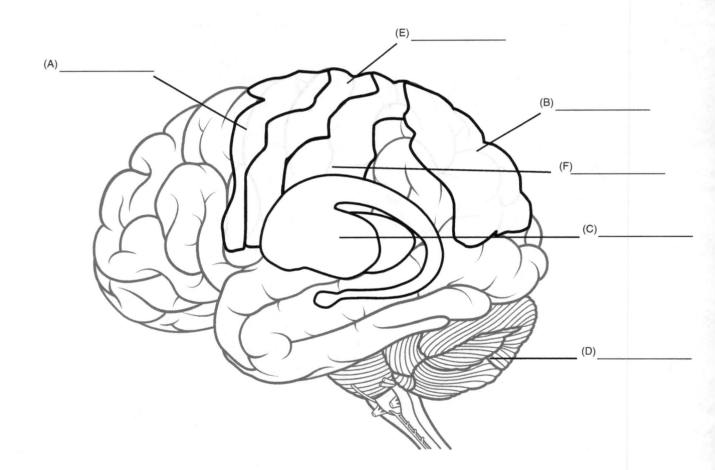

7.6 THE BASAL GANGLIA

INTRODUCTION

The basal ganglia are important in selecting the movements required for a particular action. The striatum, consisting of the caudate nucleus and the putamen in primates, forms the main input stage of the basal ganglia, receiving information from all areas of the cortex and from the limbic system. It projects via two separate pathways to the output stage, which consists of the globus pallidus and the substantia nigra, and thence to the thalamus, which loops back to the cortex.

COLOURING NOTES 7.6

Colour and label the following:

☐ Caudate nucleus (purple)
☐ Putamen (orange)
☐ Globus pallidus (lateral part) (green)

☐ Globus pallidus (medial part) (green)
☐ Substantia nigra (red)
☐ Thalamus (blue)

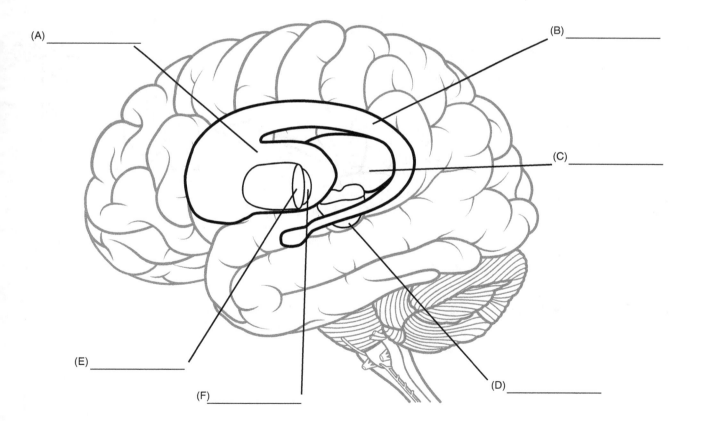

(A) _____

(B) _____

(C) _____

(D) _____

(E) _____

(F) _____

7.7 THE CEREBELLUM

INTRODUCTION

The cerebellum is part of the hindbrain and contains more than half of the total number of cells in the entire brain. Like the forebrain, it consists mainly of a highly folded cortex. The cerebellum is responsible for the learning and 'automation' of complex movements. It works with the posterior parietal cortex to develop and monitor forward plans, and it ensures that directional information from different sensory systems is correctly aligned.

—————————— COLOURING NOTES 7.7 ——————————

☐ Identify and label the cerebellum and cerebellar cortical fold
☐ Colour the cerebellum pink

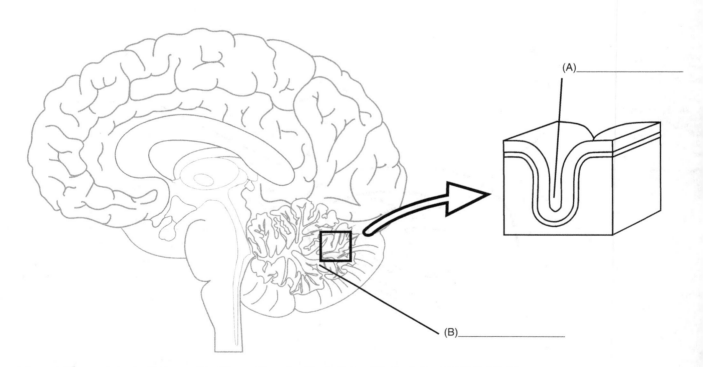

(A)_____

(B)_____

Adapted from original art created by Tomasikiewicz/Body Scientific Intl. for SAGE Publishing

7.8 CROSS SECTION THROUGH THE CEREBELLAR CORTEX

INTRODUCTION

The cerebellar cortex has a regular structure consisting of three layers (molecular layer, Purkinje cell layer and granular layer). The deepest layer contains the granule cells. The axons of each granule cell project up through the cortex to the surface layer, where they split into two 'parallel fibres' running in opposite directions parallel to the cortical surface. The middle layer contains the cell bodies of Purkinje cells. The dendrites of the Purkinje cells project up into the surface layer where they form very flat dendritic trees at right angles to the parallel fibres. Mossy fibres carry sensory input from the cortex and spinal cord and form excitatory synapses with granule cells. Climbing fibres, originating in the inferior olive and carrying information from the cortex, form excitatory synapses with the cell bodies of Purkinje cells.

COLOURING NOTES 7.8

Colour and label the following:

- ☐ Molecular layer
- ☐ Purkinje cell layer
- ☐ Granular layer
- ☐ Granule cells (blue)

- ☐ Parallel fibres (yellow)
- ☐ Purkinje cells (orange)
- ☐ Mossy fibres (purple)
- ☐ Climbing fibres (red)

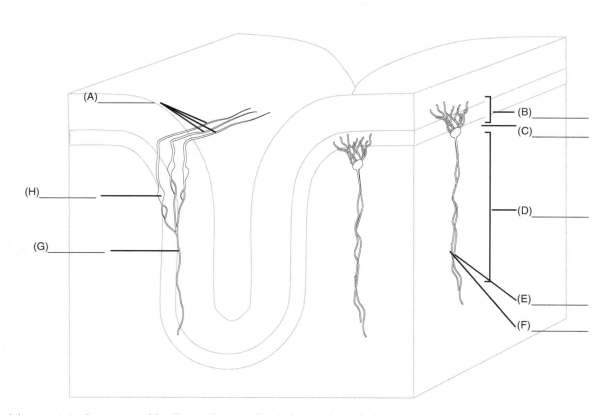

Adapted from original art created by Tomasikiewicz/Body Scientific Intl. for SAGE Publishing

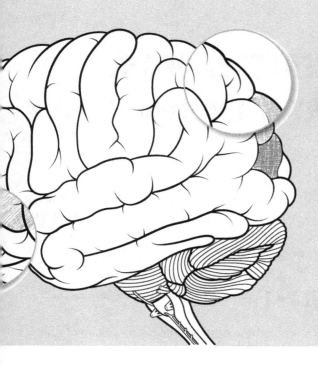

CHAPTER 8

EMOTIONAL BEHAVIOURS

INTRODUCTION

We can sense the world and act upon it but these processes do not occur in a purely reflexive and automatic way. Both sensation and action, at least in humans, are emotional in nature. We have all experienced emotions. The feelings of happiness, sadness, anger and other emotions are almost a constant experience in our lives, and they undoubtedly impact upon our behaviour. Sometimes this can be to the detriment of normal behaviour. For example, the mood disorders, such as depression, are characterised by abnormal control of mood, and hence abnormal emotional behaviour. This emphasis on emotional behaviour presents an insight into the fact that emotions are more than simply the subjective feeling that we experience. While such conscious feelings are perhaps the most prominent manifestation of emotion, they are accompanied by a multitude of other bodily responses. These include psychological changes, in both behavioural and cognitive domains, as well as more biological responses. This chapter will help you review some of the major concepts/ideas related to emotional behaviours. Remember to review Chapter 8 of *Biological Psychology*.

Answers to the labelling exercises can be found at the back of the book.

8.1 SCHEMATIC REPRESENTATION OF THE JAMES-LANGE THEORY OF EMOTION

INTRODUCTION

James-Lange theory presents a specific way of thinking about the relationship between the biological emotional responses (e.g. behavioural and physiological responses) and the subjective emotional feeling. Other theories are Cannon-Bard theory and Schachter-Singer theory. Within the context of fear, William James used the example of a man encountering a bear and both running away and feeling scared.

―――――――――――――――――― **COLOURING NOTES 8.1** ――――――――――――――――――

Label the event boxes and draw the correct direction of arrows between them to describe the process of emotional experience as proposed by James-Lange theory:

☐ Black arrows to denote processes that are common to both other theories
☐ Blue arrows to represent processes that are common to one other theory
☐ Red arrows for processes unique to this theory

Use different colours to distinguish where each event occurs:

☐ Environment (green)
☐ Brain (orange)
☐ Body (brown)

1_____

2_____

3_____

4_____

5_____

8.2 SCHEMATIC REPRESENTATION OF THE CANNON-BARD THEORY OF EMOTION

INTRODUCTION

Walter Cannon presented in 1927 an extensive critique of James-Lange theory, which culminated in the proposal of an alternative theory of the relationship between emotional responses and emotional feelings, known as Cannon-Bard theory. Cannon identified issues with James-Lange theory in terms of the speed, sensitivity and specificity of the emotional responses. There is also the Schachter-Singer theory of emotion.

—— COLOURING NOTES 8.2 ——

Label the event boxes and draw the correct direction of arrows between them to describe the process of emotional experience as proposed by Cannon-Bard theory:

☐ Black arrows to denote processes that are common to both other theories
☐ Blue arrows to represent processes that are common to one other theory
☐ Red arrows for processes unique to this theory

Use different colours to distinguish where each event occurs:

☐ Environment (green)
☐ Brain (orange)
☐ Body (brown)

1_____

2_____

3_____

4_____

8.3 SCHEMATIC REPRESENTATION OF THE SCHACHTER-SINGER THEORY OF EMOTION

INTRODUCTION

Schacter and Singer presented a more recent theory concerning the relationship between emotional responses and emotional feelings. This theory is also known as the two-factor or cognitive labelling theory. The proposal of the theory is linked to a famous study that gave participants adrenaline under the false guise of a novel vitamin supplement 'Suproxin' and then influenced their emotional experience by using actors.

--- **COLOURING NOTES 8.3** ---

Label the event boxes and draw the correct direction of arrows between them to describe the process of emotional experience as proposed by Schachter-Singer theory:

☐ Black arrows to denote processes that are common to both other theories
☐ Blue arrows to represent processes that are common to one other theory
☐ Red arrows for processes unique to this theory

Use different colours to distinguish where each event occurs:

☐ Environment (green)
☐ Brain (orange)
☐ Body (brown)

1_____

2_____

3_____

4_____

5_____

6_____

7_____

8.4 REPRESENTATION OF THE LIMBIC SYSTEM

INTRODUCTION

The limbic system is historically used to describe the areas of the brain that are involved in emotional processing. As understanding has progressed, brain areas have been included or removed from the limbic system, meaning that while it remains an accurate answer to the question 'what brain areas are involved in emotion?', it is not a particularly useful answer. Instead, it is more helpful to focus on individual brain areas that comprise the limbic system.

--- **COLOURING NOTES 8.4** ---

Key components of the limbic system are indicated. Label and colour:

☐ The amygdala (red)
☐ The cingulate gyrus (green)
☐ The prefrontal cortex (yellow)
☐ The hypothalamus (blue)

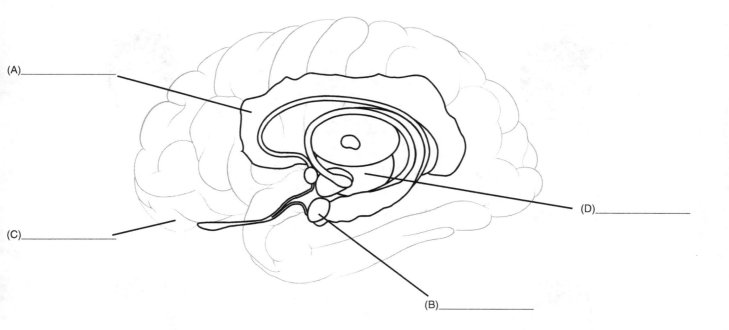

8.5 CORE EMOTIONAL FACIAL EXPRESSIONS

INTRODUCTION

There are a number of ways in which we can express our emotional state. These consist of changes in our posture, the sounds that we make and facial expressions. Facial expressions are the most easily recognisable and distinct across emotions. There are a number of core emotions that are defined by their distinct facial expressions. There is agreement on six of these (anger, sadness, happiness, fear, disgust and surprise). It is important that emotional states are communicated in a consistent and rapidly detectable manner. Socially in humans, it tells us how others feel and so how they might react to certain situations. For example, we would be much less likely to challenge someone who appears to be in an aggressive state than one who is in a fearful state. In this way, we can avoid confrontation and potential danger.

COLOURING NOTES 8.5

Assign the correct label to the facial expression communicating the following emotions:

☐ Anger
☐ Sadness
☐ Happiness
☐ Fear
☐ Disgust
☐ Surprise

(A)_____

(B)_____

(C)_____

(D)_____

(E)_____

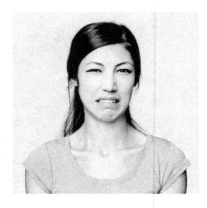

(F)_____

8.6 THE HYPOTHALAMIC-PITUITARY-ADRENAL AXIS

INTRODUCTION

The hypothalamic-pituitary-adrenal (HPA) axis regulates stress responses. Dysregulation of the HPA is apparent in posttraumatic stress disorder. While cortisol levels are low, corticotropin-releasing factor is high in PTSD. The key to this lies in the feedback that cortisol has on its own release.

COLOURING NOTES 8.6

Label and colour:

☐ The hypothalamus (blue)
☐ The pituitary gland (red)
☐ The adrenal cortex (yellow)

Label and colour the released hormones:

☐ CRF (green)
☐ ACTH (brown)
☐ Cortisol (orange)

Draw the feedback loop that cortisol exerts on its own release

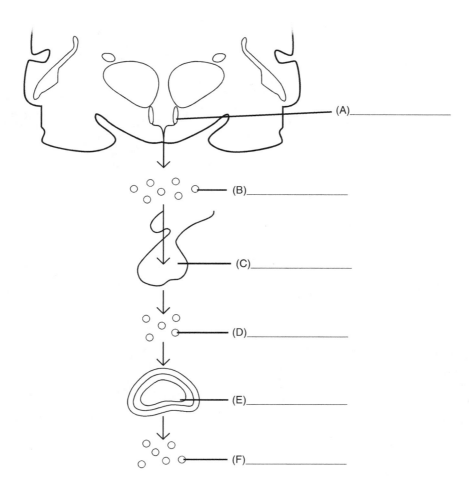

Adapted from Hyman, S.E. (1969). 'How adversity gets under the skin', *Nature Neuroscience*. With permission from the Copyright Clearance Center: Springer Nature.

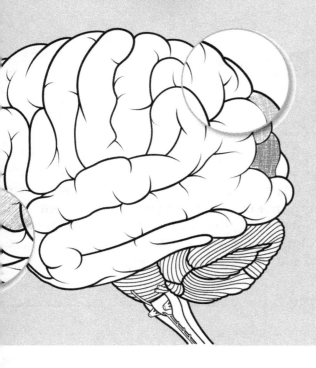

CHAPTER 9

MOTIVATED BEHAVIOURS

INTRODUCTION

Behaviour is frequently activated by and directed towards or away from particular objects. These stimuli hold their influence over behaviour because they possess motivational properties. Importantly, these properties are often learned through prior experience. For example, a cue that predicts a painful or traumatic outcome will come to elicit anxiety or fear, and would lead to us avoiding contact with the cue. Similarly, a cue that is predictive of food, or even illicit drugs, will be automatically approached and will trigger more positive emotional responses. By understanding the biological bases of motivational processes we can gain greater insight into motivated behaviours (e.g. eating and sleep), as well as abnormally exaggerated responses and behaviours (e.g. sleep disorders and eating disorders). This chapter will help you review the biological bases of eating and sleep. Remember to review Chapter 9 of *Biological Psychology*.

Answers to the labelling exercises can be found at the back of the book.

9.1 DIGESTIVE SYSTEM

INTRODUCTION

We need to eat food to provide the energy that our bodies need to function and motivational processes govern what and how much we eat, but to use the energy from food we have to get it inside the body in a usable form. When we eat, food is broken down into its constituent parts so that the useful bits (nutrients) can be absorbed from the gut and the bits that cannot be used by the body are excreted. The absorption of nutrients into the bloodstream from the digested food provides energy and essential other materials for the body to function. Signals from areas within the digestive (or gastrointestinal) system are used to monitor the likely levels of nutrients that will be absorbed and so affect eating.

COLOURING NOTES 9.1

Label and colour:

- ☐ The oesophagus (pink)
- ☐ The stomach (red)
- ☐ The liver (brown)

- ☐ The duodenum (pink)
- ☐ The small intestine (orange)
- ☐ The large intestine (green)

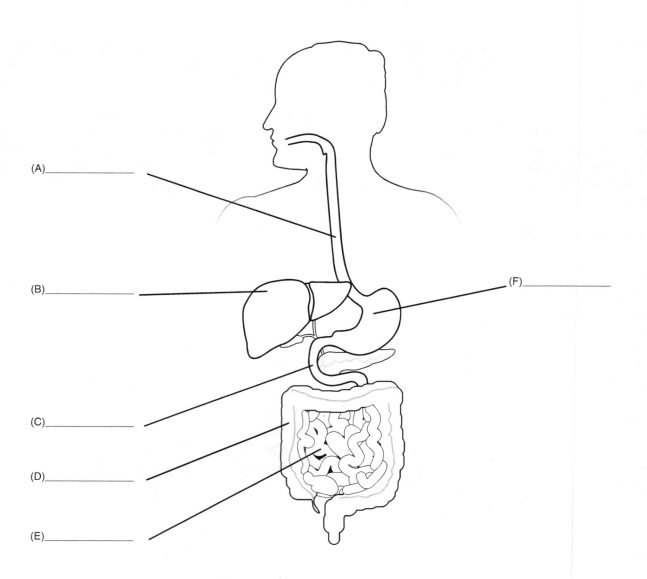

(A)_____

(B)_____

(C)_____

(D)_____

(E)_____

(F)_____

9.2 HYPOTHALAMIC NUCLEI INVOLVED IN EATING

INTRODUCTION

The brain receives information continuously about food that is being eaten and nutrients that are circulating and being stored. We are able to sense nutrients at various stages of digestion, absorption and metabolism and send information about these nutrients to the brain. Once this information reaches the brain there is further processing and integration with other inputs relevant to eating so that motor outputs (eating behaviours) are generated. There are complex neural systems involved in appetite but an area of the brain that has received attention in research is the hypothalamus. The hypothalamus comprises a number of subdivisions or 'nuclei', some of which play an important role in eating. These are the paraventricular nucleus (PVN), arcuate nucleus (ARC) and lateral hypothalamus (LH). By the release of neuropeptides, signals are sent between these nuclei that lead to either the promotion or inhibition of eating.

––––––––––––––––– **COLOURING NOTES 9.2** –––––––––––––––––

Label and colour:

☐ The PVN (green)
☐ The ARC (yellow)
☐ The LH (orange)

Write in the relevant nucleus where neurons that express NPY, AgRP, α MSH and POMC are located

Draw coloured arrows to show the projection where NPY, AgRP and α MSH are released:

☐ Red to denote activation of the target area
☐ Blue to denote inhibition of the target area

Draw coloured arrows from relevant nuclei to show:

☐ Which nucleus is involved in the promotion of eating (red)
☐ Which nucleus is involved in the inhibition of eating (blue)

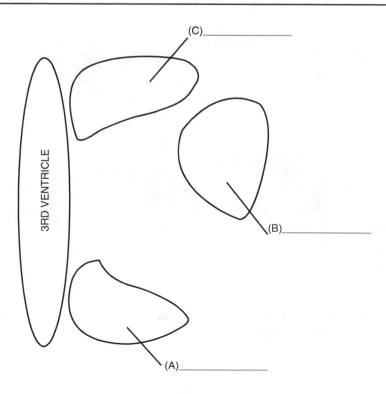

9.3 AFFECTIVE REACTIONS TO TASTE

INTRODUCTION

Responses to some basic tastes have an unlearned or innate component. So, human babies have a positive affective reaction to sweet tastes and a negative affective reaction to bitter tastes. This is probably because these reactions serve to ensure the acceptance of milk and the rejection of poisons and so are adaptive. However, our initial responses to tastes can be readily modified via experience, such that we can come to like some bitter-tasting foods if we learn that they are not actually dangerous. Some of this learning occurs socially as we observe the eating patterns of others allowing for social and cultural influences on food choice.

───────────────── **COLOURING NOTES 9.3** ─────────────────

Assign the correct label to the facial expressions elicited in response to:

☐ Control (normal)
☐ Bitter
☐ Sweet
☐ Sour

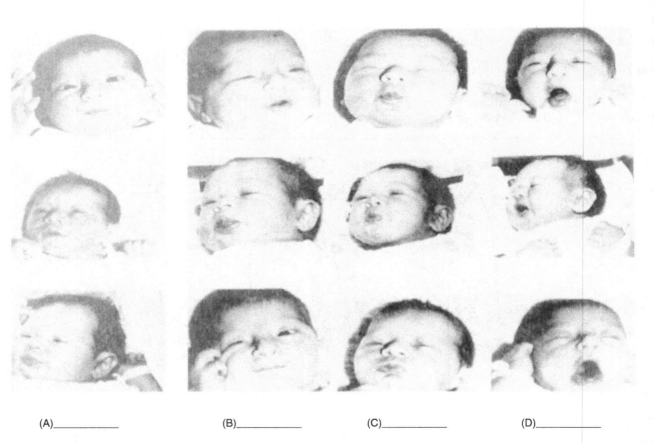

(A)_____   (B)_____   (C)_____   (D)_____

Source: Image courtesy of Weiffenbach (1977). *Taste and Development.* © U.S. Department of Health, Education, and Welfare, Public Health Service, National Institutes of Health.

9.4 THE MESOLIMBIC AND MESOCORTICAL DOPAMINE SYSTEM

INTRODUCTION

Dopamine is an important neurotransmitter in the regulation of motivated behaviours. A rich source of dopamine neurons is the ventral tegmental area (VTA) in the midbrain. From here, projections are sent to the limbic and cortical areas of the brain, which thus create the mesolimbic and mesocortical dopamine systems. Dopamine release in the striatum (nucleus accumbens) is linked to motivational 'wanting', and the targets of the mesolimbic and mesocortical dopamine systems are activated by food-related images.

COLOURING NOTES 9.4

Label and colour:

☐ The VTA (green)
☐ The nucleus accumbens (purple)
☐ The amygdala (blue)

Label and colour the arrows showing the direction of the mesolimbic (red) and mesocortical (light blue) projections

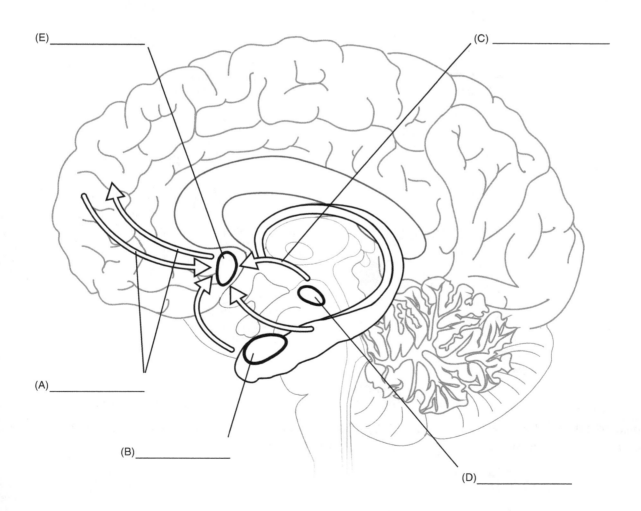

(E)_____

(C)_____

(A)_____

(B)_____

(D)_____

Adapted from original created by Christina Wheeler/Body Scientific Intl. for Sage Publishing.

9.5 EEG PATTERNS OBSERVED DURING WAKING AND SLEEP

INTRODUCTION

The pattern of brain activity that is recorded via electroencephalography (EEG) varies across the course of sleep. Sleep can thus be broken down into different stages (1–4 + REM sleep), which have distinct EEG patterns.

COLOURING NOTES 9.5

Label (at the top) and colour the background for each distinct EEG pattern:

☐ Awake [already labelled for you] (red)
☐ Stage 1 (blue)
☐ Stage 2 (yellow)
☐ Stages 3-4 (green)

Colour in red and label the background for the pattern that is similar to waking

Below the EEG trace indicate with horizontal black lines the relative level of consciousness for each stage of sleep.

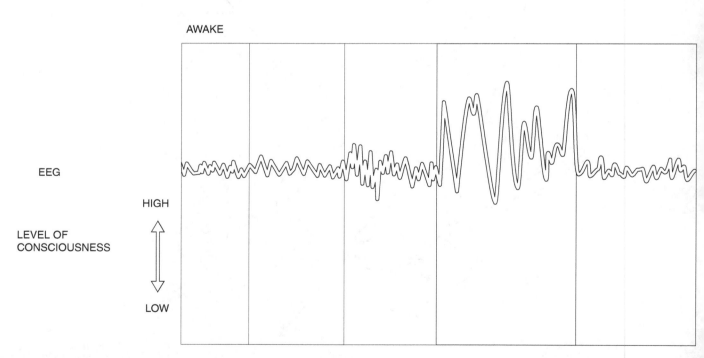

Adapted from Bryant, P.A., et al. (2004). 'Sick and tired: does sleep have a vital role in the immune system?', *Nature Reviews Immunology*. With permission from the Copyright Clearance Centre: Springer Nature.

9.6 SLEEP STAGES DURING ONE NIGHT

INTRODUCTION

After a person has fallen asleep, there is progress through the different stages of sleep and REM sleep throughout the night in cycles that alternate between periods of REM and non-REM sleep that take about 90 minutes.

––––––––––––––––––––––––––– **COLOURING NOTES 9.6** –––––––––––––––––––––––––––

Label on the y axis of the graph:

☐ Awakening
☐ Stage 1
☐ Stage 2
☐ Stage 3
☐ Stage 4
☐ REM sleep

Colour:

☐ The periods of REM and brief awakening (green)
☐ The period of SWS (grey)

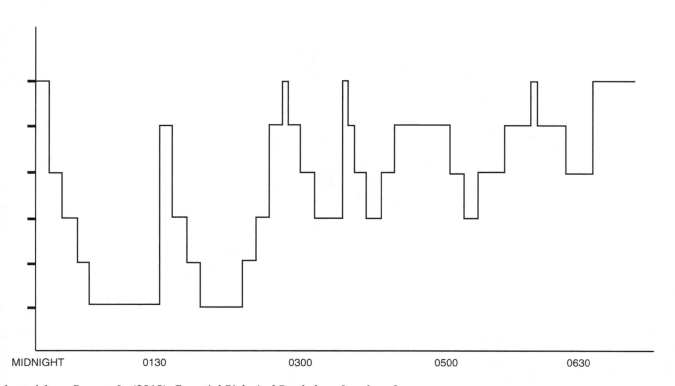

Adapted from Barnes, J., (2013). *Essential Biological Psychology*. London: Sage.

9.7 BRAIN AREAS INVOLVED IN WAKING

INTRODUCTION

The brain mechanisms of waking involve two main pathways that form an ascending arousal system. These pathways provide wide stimulation of the cortex to produce the desynchronised EEG that is characteristic of the waking state.

COLOURING NOTES 9.7

Label and colour:

☐ The PPT/LDT (green)
☐ The thalamus (yellow)
☐ The cortex (pink)
☐ The basal forebrain (brown)
☐ Lateral hypothalamus (red)
☐ The monoaminergic brainstem (purple)
☐ The brainstem-thalamus-cortex pathway (blue) and the monoamine-lateral hypothalamus/basal forebrain-cortex pathway (orange)

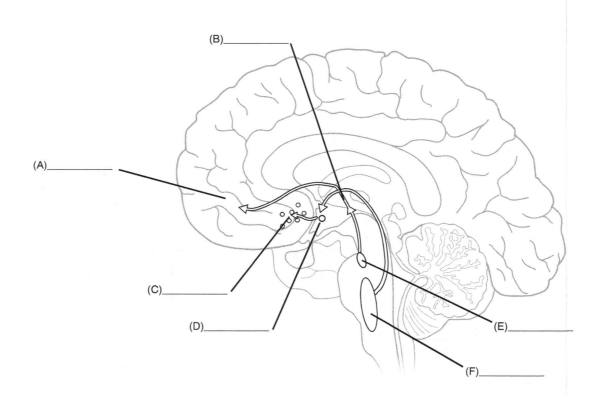

9.8 BRAIN AREAS INVOLVED IN SLEEP

INTRODUCTION

One area of the brain that is more active during sleep than wakefulness is the ventrolateral preoptic nucleus (VLPO). Neurons in this region of the hypothalamus contain the inhibitory neurotransmitters GABA and they connect with the monoaminergic arousal systems in the hypothalamus and brainstem. When the VLPO is damaged, it causes insomnia. This evidence suggests that projections from the VLPO form a sleep-promoting pathway that inhibits arousal systems.

COLOURING NOTES 9.8

Label and colour:

☐ The ventrolateral preoptic nucleus (blue)
☐ The monoaminergic brainstem (purple)
☐ The thalamus (yellow)
☐ The cortex (pink)
☐ The basal forebrain (brown)
☐ The lateral hypothalamus (red)
☐ The PPT/LDT (green)

Colour:

☐ The inhibitory projections from the VLPO that inhibit arousal systems (orange)

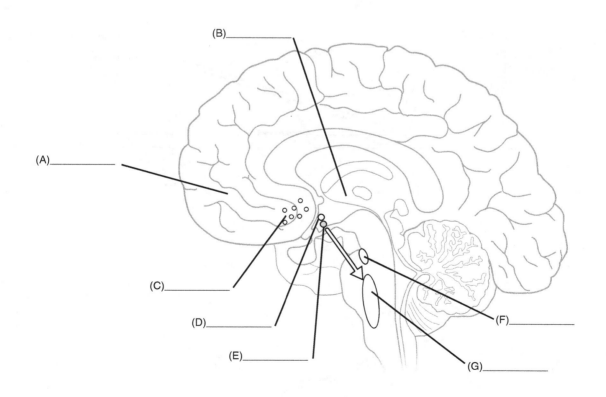

9.9 A SCHEMATIC OF THE FLIP-FLOP MECHANISM THAT CONTROLS SHIFTS BETWEEN SLEEPING AND WAKING

INTRODUCTION

While there is clearly an interaction between the brain areas involved in sleep and waking, the transition between the two states still needs to be explained. The current understanding is that there are 'flip-flop' switches that allow fast and complete transitions from waking to sleep and vice versa. In the brain, these flip-flops seem be made up of groups of neurons that inhibit each other. The primary groups of neurons involved are in the VLPO.

COLOURING NOTES 9.9

Label and colour:

☐ The VLPO (blue)
☐ The monoaminergic brainstem (yellow)
☐ The orexin system (orange)

Draw:

☐ Activating projections in green
☐ Inhibitory projections in red

(A)

AWAKE

ON

(B)

SLEEP

OFF

Adapted with permission of Wiley. From Saper et al. (2005). 'Homeostatic, circadian, and emotional regulation of sleep', *Journal of Comparative Neurology*, 493(1). Permission conveyed through Copyright Clearance Center, Inc.

ANSWERS

CHAPTER 1

COLOURING NOTES 1.1

(a) Brain
(b) Spinal cord
(c) Nerves

The central nervous system is inclusive of the brain and spinal cord, whilst the nerves make up the peripheral nervous system.

COLOURING NOTES 1.2

(a) Superior
(b) Proximal
(c) Distal
(d) Medial
(e) Lateral
(f) Inferior

COLOURING NOTES 1.3

(a) Anterior
(b) Superior
(c) Posterior
(d) Inferior
(e) Coronal
(f) Sagittal
(g) Horizontal

COLOURING NOTES 1.4

(a) Left cerebral hemisphere
(b) Right cerebral hemisphere
(c) Cerebellum (this appears in both images)
(d) Brainstem

COLOURING NOTES 1.5

(a) Central sulcus
(b) Parietal lobe
(c) Occipital lobe
(d) Cerebellum
(e) Spinal cord
(f) Brainstem
(g) Temporal lobe
(h) Lateral fissure
(i) Frontal lobe

COLOURING NOTES 1.6

(a) Pons
(b) Medulla
(c) Midbrain
(d) Hindbrain

COLOURING NOTES 1.7

(a) Afferent
(b) Soma of sensory neuron
(c) Grey matter
(d) White matter
(e) Dorsal root
(f) Spinal nerve
(g) Ventral root
(h) Soma of motor neuron
(i) Efferent

COLOURING NOTES 1.8

(a) Lateral ventricles
(b) Third ventricle
(c) Cerebral aqueduct
(d) Fourth ventricle
(e) Central canal of spinal cord

CHAPTER 2

COLOURING NOTES 2.1

(a) Dendrites
(b) Nucleus
(c) Axon
(d) Cell body
(e) Schwann cells
(f) Axon terminals
(g) Myelin sheath

COLOURING NOTES 2.2

(a) Myelin sheath
(b) Node of Ranvier
(c) Axon
(d) Schwann cell
(e) Oligodendrocyte
(f) Axon

COLOURING NOTES 2.3

(a) Phospholipids
(b) Protein channels
(c) Extracellular fluid
(d) Intracellular fluid

COLOURING NOTES 2.4

(a) K+ ion channel
(b) Na+K+–ATPase transporter
(c) Inside neuron
(d) Outside neuron

Image needs to be recreated for answers with the labels added in

COLOURING NOTES 2.5

(a) Threshold line
(b) Depolarisation
(c) Repolarisation
(d) Stimulus
(e) Resting potential line

COLOURING NOTES 2.6

(a) Presynaptic axon
(b) Postsynaptic axon
(c) Axon terminal
(d) Synaptic cleft
(e) Dendrites
(f) Presynaptic neuron

(g) Postsynaptic neuron
(h) Axon

COLOURING NOTES 2.7

(a) Axon
(b) Synaptic vesicle
(c) Dendrite
(d) Synaptic cleft
(e) Neurotransmitter

COLOURING NOTES 2.8

(a) Synapatic cleft
(b) Vesicle
(c) Cytoplasm
(d) Neurotransmitter molecules

COLOURING NOTES 2.9

(a) Axon terminal
(b) Neurotransmitter transporter
(c) Postsynaptic receptor
(d) Synaptic vesicle
(e) Neurotransmitter
(f) Synaptic cleft
(g) Dendrite

COLOURING NOTES 2.10

(a) Synaptic cleft
(b) Presynaptic terminal
(c) Postsynaptic terminal
(d) Receptors
(e) Neurotransmitter
(f) Astrocyte
(g) Synaptic vesicle

COLOURING NOTES 2.11

Amino acids	Neuropeptides
GABA	Opioids
Glutamate	Neuropeptide Y
Glycine	Orexin
	Cholecystokinin

Monoamines	
Serotonin	**Lipids/gasesGAB**
Dopamine	Cannabinoids
Histamine	Nitric oxide
Noradrenaline	

CHAPTER 3

COLOURING NOTES 3.1

Inhalation will be the method presenting the earliest peak of concentration of drug in the brain, with injection following soon after and both will be quite high peaks. After that, snorting/snuffing follows but is a much lower peak. Finally, Ingestion is last to peak with a much wider but flatter curve. See *The Brain: Understanding Neurobiology Through the Study of Addiction*, https://science.education.nih.gov/supplements/nih_neuro.pdf.

COLOURING NOTES 3.2

(a) Agonist
(b) Antagonist
(c) Partial inverse agonist

COLOURING NOTES 3.3

(a) Therapeutic effect
(b) Therapeutic index
(c) Toxic effect

COLOURING NOTES 3.4

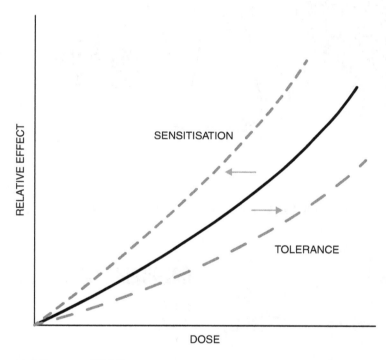

Adapted from Hilal-Dandan and Brunton (2014)

COLOURING NOTES 3.5

(a) No effect
(b) Giddy
(c) Sleep
(d) Unconscious
(e) Laboured breathing
(f) Death

COLOURING NOTES 3.6 (A)

(a) Neurotransmitter
(b) Ion
(c) Closed ion channel
(d) Ionotropic receptor

COLOURING NOTES 3.6 (B)

(a) Neurotransmitter
(b) Metabotropic receptor
(c) G-protein
(d) G-protein gated ion channel

COLOURING NOTES 3.7

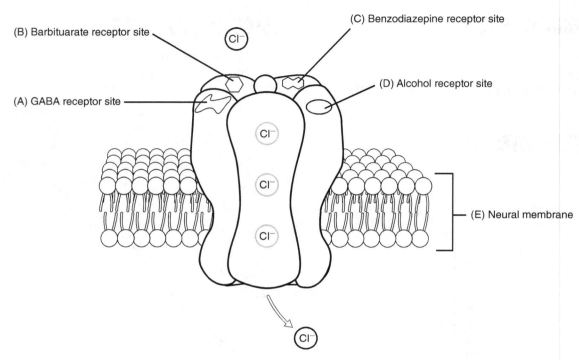

Adapted from original created by Carolina Hrejsa/Body Scientific Intl. for Sage Publishing.

COLOURING NOTES 3.8

(a) Cocaine
(b) Presynaptic transporter protein
(c) Dopamine

COLOURING NOTES 3.9

(a) Postsynaptic receptors
(b) Endogenous opioids
(c) Morphine

COLOURING NOTES 3.10

(a) Nicotine
(b) Acetylcholine
(c) Axon terminal
(d) Acetylcholine receptors

COLOURING NOTES 3.11

(a) Adenosine
(b) Caffeine

CHAPTER 4

COLOURING NOTES 4.1

(a) Sugar-phosphate backbone

1. A
2. G
3. T
4. C
5. T
6. G
7. C
8. A

COLOURING NOTES 4.2 (A)

(a) Homologous chromosome
(b) Sister chromatids
(c) Homologues separate, sisters remain attached
(d) Sisters separate
(e) DNA replication recombination
(f) Chromosome segregation (meiosis I)
(g) Chromosome segregation (meiosis II)
(h) Gametes

COLOURING NOTES 4.2 (B)

(a) Interphase
(b) Prophase
(c) Metaphase
(d) Anaphase
(e) Telophase

COLOURING NOTES 4.3

(a) Neural plate
(b) Non-neural ectoderm
(c) Neural groove
(d) Neural tube

COLOURING NOTES 4.4

(a) Forebrain
(b) Midbrain
(c) Hindbrain
(d) Forebrain

(e) Spinal cord
(f) Midbrain
(g) Hindbrain
(h) Cranial nerves
(i) Forebrain
(j) Spinal cord
(k) Midbrain
(l) Hindbrain
(m) Spinal cord
(n) Forebrain
(o) Midbrain (hidden)
(p) Hindbrain
(q) Spinal cord

COLOURING NOTES 4.5

(a) Ventricular zone
(b) Cortical plate
(c) Brain surface
(d) The radial glia
(e) The fluid-filled ventricle

The cells (circles) in the cortical plate (B) that are closest to the ventricular zone (A) should be yellow. The cells (circles) closest to the brain surface (C) should be pink.

COLOURING NOTES 4.6

(a) Migration zone
(b) Outer layer of the brain (where the oldest neurons are)
(c) Ventricular zone (where the youngest neurons are)
(d) Migrating neurons
(e) Radial glial fibres

COLOURING NOTES 4.7

(a) Cell body
(b) Axon
(c) Growth cone

The BioPsychology Colouring Book, published 2021 by SAGE Publishing. © Suzanne Higgs, Alison Cooper and Jonathan Lee, 2021

COLOURING NOTES 4.8

(a) Cell breaks into apoptotic bodies
(b) Nuclear collapse
(c) Normal cell
   (i) cytoplasm
   (ii) nucleus
   (iii) other organelles
(d) Cell damage
(e) Cell parts phagocytosed
(f) Cell shrinks developing buds or blebs

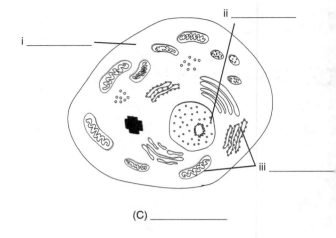

(C) _____

COLOURING NOTES 4.9

(a) Caudate
(b) Putamen
(c) Healthy brain
(d) Parkinson's disease
(e) Substantia nigra pars compacta

The nigrostriatal pathways should go from the caudate and putamen down to the substansia nigra pars compacta.

COLOURING NOTES 4.10

(a) Caudate
(b) Putamen
(c) Healthy brain
(d) Brain with Huntington's disease

COLOURING NOTES 4.11

(a) Tyrosine
(b) L-DOPA

(c) Dopamine
(d) Presynaptic neuron
(e) Postsynaptic neuron
(f) Synaptic cleft
(g) Vesicles containing dopamine
(h) Dopamine receptors

COLOURING NOTES 4.12

Note on answers: Some of these are interchangeable.

(a), (b) and (c) are dopamine, 5-HT and GABA – in any order
(d) and (e) can be either GABA or COMT so long as GABA is with synthesis and COMT is with degradation
(f) Dysbindin
(g) and (h) can be either synthesis or degradation so long as degradation is with COMT and synthesis is with GABA
(i) Release
(j) DISC1

CHAPTER 5

COLOURING NOTES 5.1

Panel A – screens are 1 & 3; processors are 2 & 4.

Panel B – 2 & 4 should be coloured.

Panel C – 1 should be coloured as the screen could still have power to it.

Circling exercises:

(a) The images that represent a double dissociation are B1 and B2; and C1 and C2
(b) The images that represent a single dissociation are B3 and B4; and C3 and C4

COLOURING NOTES 5.2

(a) Memory strength
(b) Amount learned on trial
(c) Prediction error

Your lines may look a little something like this:

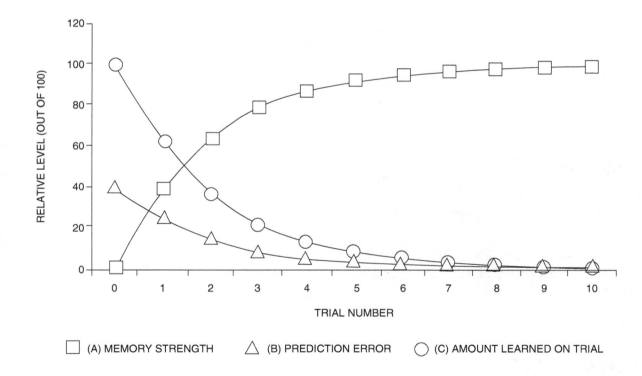

COLOURING NOTES 5.3

(a) Occipital lobe – more perceptual neurons
(b) Temporal lobe – more mnemonic neurons

The red arrow should go from the occipital lobe towards the temporal lobe.

COLOURING NOTES 5.4

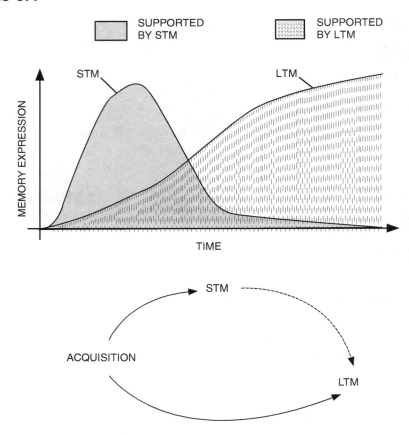

COLOURING NOTES 5.5

(a) Output neuron
(b) and (c) Input neurons. Strong vs. weak could be either way round.

COLOURING NOTES 5.6

(a) The output neuron
(b) The input neuronal cell body
(c) The interneuron

Axonal projection is from B to 3
Interneuron projections are B to 1 and C to 2
Excitatory synapses are 1 and 3
Inhibitory synapse is 2
3 is strengthened by LTP

COLOURING NOTES 5.7

(a) The output neuron
(b) The input neuronal cell body
(c) The interneuron

Axonal projection from input to output is from B to 3.
Axonal projection from input to interneuron is from B to 1.
Axonal projection from interneuron to output is from C to 2.
Excitatory synapses are 1 and 3.
Inhibitory synapse is 2.
1 is weakened by LTD.
C has reduced activity.

COLOURING NOTES 5.8

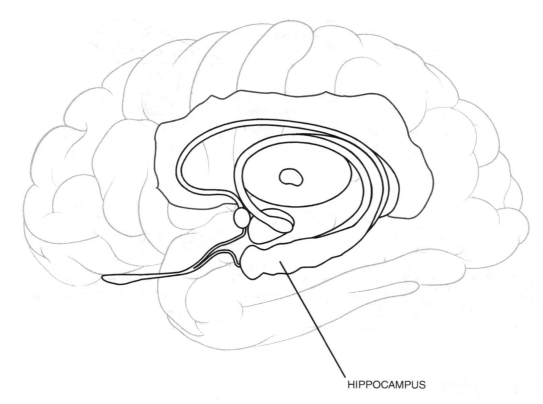

HIPPOCAMPUS

Adapted from original creation by Hrejsa/Body Scientific Intl. for SAGE Publishing

COLOURING NOTES 5.9

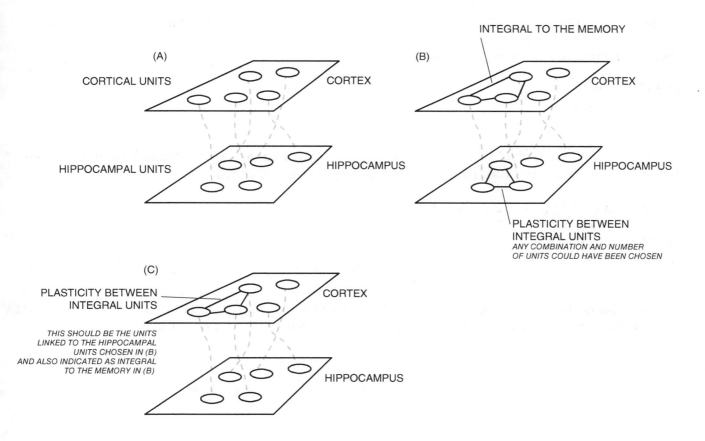

(A)

CORTICAL UNITS   CORTEX

HIPPOCAMPAL UNITS   HIPPOCAMPUS

(B)

INTEGRAL TO THE MEMORY

CORTEX

HIPPOCAMPUS

PLASTICITY BETWEEN
INTEGRAL UNITS
*ANY COMBINATION AND NUMBER
OF UNITS COULD HAVE BEEN CHOSEN*

(C)

PLASTICITY BETWEEN
INTEGRAL UNITS   CORTEX

*THIS SHOULD BE THE UNITS
LINKED TO THE HIPPOCAMPAL
UNITS CHOSEN IN (B)
AND ALSO INDICATED AS INTEGRAL
TO THE MEMORY IN (B)*

HIPPOCAMPUS

COLOURING NOTES 5.10

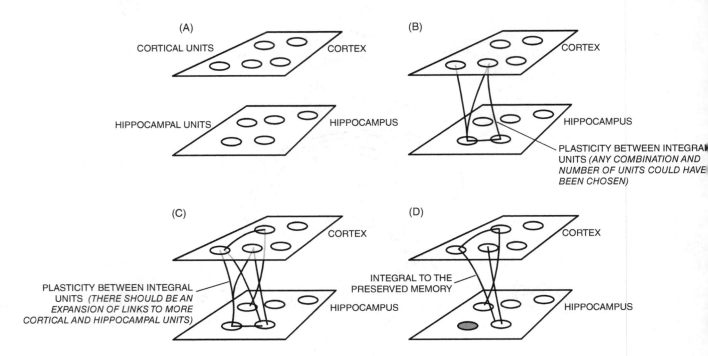

COLOURING NOTES 5.11

Before extinction:

(a) Infralimbic cortex
(b) Hippocampus
(c) Amygdala

In this scenario the CS should only have an arrow to the amygdala and the fear response is activated.

After extinction – in the extinction context:

(d) Infralimbic cortex
(e) Hippocampus
(f) Amygdala

In this scenario the CS should have arrows to all three brain areas and there should be a line between the infralimbic cortex and the amygdala. The fear response is not activated.

After extinction – in a different context:

(g) Infralimbic cortex
(h) Hippocampus
(i) Amygdala

In this scenario, there should be arrows from the CS to all three brain areas, but this time, there should be an arrow between the hippocampus and the infralimbic cortex. The fear response is activated.

CHAPTER 6

COLOURING NOTES 6.1

(a) Iris
(b) Cornea
(c) Pupil
(d) Lens
(e) Retina
(f) Optic nerve

COLOURING NOTES 6.2

(a) Cornea
(b) Iris
(c) Lens
(d) Retina
(e) Optic nerve
(f) Pupil
(g) Fixation point
(h) Light

COLOURING NOTES 6.3

(a) Macula
(b) Fovea
(c) Retina
(d) Vitreous gel
(e) Optic nerve
(f) Iris
(g) Cornea
(h) Pupil
(i) Lens
(j) Bipolar cell
(k) Amacrine cell
(l) Cone
(m) Horizontal cell
(n) Ganglion cell
(o) Rod

COLOURING NOTES 6.4

(a) Cell bodies
(b) Cone photoreceptors
(c) Rod photoreceptors
(d) Synaptic terminals
(e) Inner segments
(f) Outer segments
(g) Membranous discs containing photo pigments

COLOURING NOTES 6.5

(a) On responses
(b) Off responses

COLOURING NOTES 6.6

(a) Left visual field
(b) Right visual field
(c) Temporal
(d) Nasal
(e) Optic chiasma
(f) Lateral geniculate nucleus
(g) Optic radiation
(h) Primary visual cortex
(i) Superior colliculus

COLOURING NOTES 6.7

(a) Parietal cortex
(b) Inferotemporal cortex
(c) Dorsal stream
(d) Ventral stream

COLOURING NOTES 6.8

(a) Outer ear
(b) Middle ear
(c) Inner ear
(d) Auditory nerve
(e) Cochlea
(f) Eustachian tube
(g) Ear drum
(h) Ear canal
(i) Hammer
(j) Anvil
(k) Pinna
(l) Stirrup

COLOURING NOTES 6.9

(a) Inner hair cells
(b) Tectorial membrane
(c) Outer hair cells
(d) Basilar membrane
(e) Auditory nerve
(f) Basilar membrane

COLOURING NOTES 6.10

(a) Medial geniculate body
(b) Primary auditory cortex (A1)
(c) Inferior colliculus
(d) Superior olivary nucleus
(e) Auditory nerve
(f) Cochlea

COLOURING NOTES 6.11

(a) Semicircular canals
(b) Utricle
(c) Saccule
(d) Cochlea

COLOURING NOTES 6.12

(a) Otoliths
(b) Gelatinous membrane
(c) Hair cells
(d) Neurons

COLOURING NOTES 6.13

(a) Meissner's corpuscle
(b) Merkel's disc
(c) Ruffini endings
(d) Pacinian corpuscle
(e) Free nerve endings
(f) Hair

COLOURING NOTES 6.14

(a) Cerebral cortex
(b) Midbrain
(c) Pons
(d) Medulla
(e) Medulla
(f) Spinal cord
(g) Dorsal column nuclei
(h) Dorsal root ganglion cells
(i) Medial lemniscus
(j) Ventral posterior nucleus
(k) Primary somatosensory cortex (S1)

COLOURING NOTES 6.15

(a) Midbrain
(b) Periaqueductal grey area
(c) Pons
(d) Medulla

(e) Spinal cord
(f) Endogenous opioids

COLOURING NOTES 6.16

(a) Ventral posterior medial thalamic nucleus
(b) Primary gustatory cortex
(c) Facial nerve
(d) Nucleus of the solitary tract
(e) Glossopharyngeal nerve
(f) Vagus nerve
(g) Tongue
(h) Taste receptor cell

COLOURING NOTES 6.17

(a) Taste pore
(b) Gustatory hair
(c) Gustatory receptor cell
(d) Basal cell
(e) Sensory neurons
(f) Connective tissue
(g) Supporting cell

COLOURING NOTES 6.18

(a) Olfactory bulb
(b) Cribriform formina
(c) Axon
(d) Basal cell
(e) Supporting cell
(f) Olfactory neuron
(g) Dendrite
(h) Cilia
(i) Olfactory vesicle

COLOURING NOTES 6.19

(a) Olfactory neurons
(b) Glomerulus
(c) Amygdala
(d) Entorhinal cortex
(e) Piriform cortex (the primary olfactory cortex)
(f) Mitral cells

CHAPTER 7

COLOURING NOTES 7.1

(a) Biceps contracts
(b) Triceps relaxes
(c) Biceps relaxes
(d) Triceps contracts

COLOURING NOTES 7.2

(a) Axon of motor neuron
(b) Neuromuscular junction
(c) Myofibrils
(d) Muscle fibre

COLOURING NOTES 7.3

(a) Actin filaments
(b) Myosin filaments

COLOURING NOTES 7.4

(a) Sensory cell body
(b) Spinal cord
(c) Antagonist muscle
(d) Extrafusal fibre
(e) Agonist muscle
(f) Intrafusal muscle fibres with spindle
(g) Alpha motoneuron loop
(h) Gamma motoneuron pathway
(i) Inhibitory loop

COLOURING NOTES 7.5

(a) Secondary motor cortex
(b) Posterior parietal cortex

(c) Basal ganglia
(d) Cerebellum
(e) Primary motor cortex
(f) Somatosensory cortex

COLOURING NOTES 7.6

(a) Putamen
(b) Caudate nucleus
(c) Thalamus
(d) Substantia nigra
(e) Globus pallidus (lateral part)
(f) Globus pallidus (medial part)

COLOURING NOTES 7.7

(a) Cerebellar cortical fold
(b) Cerebellum

COLOURING NOTES 7.8

(a) Parallel fibres
(b) Molecular layer
(c) Purkinje cell layer
(d) Granular layer
(e) Purkinje cells
(f) Climbing fibres
(g) Mossy fibres
(h) Granule cells

CHAPTER 8

COLOURING NOTES 8.1

1. Stimulus (environment)
2. Perception (brain)
3. Peripheral response (body)
4. Interpretation (brain)
5. Emotion (brain)

Arrows should be present between 1→2→3→4→5.

You should have black arrows between 1→2 & 2→3.

And a blue arrow between 4→5.

This leaves 3→4 as a red arrow.

COLOURING NOTES 8.2

1. Stimulus (environment)
2. Perception (brain)
3. Peripheral response (body)
4. Emotion (brain)

Arrows should be present between 1→2→3;
2→4; 4→3.

You should have black arrows between 1→2 & 2→3.

And all others should be red.

COLOURING NOTES 8.3

1. Stimulus (environment)
2. Perception (brain)
3. Peripheral response (body)
4. Context (environment)
5. Which emotion? (brain)
6. Interpretation (brain)
7. Emotion (brain)

There should be arrows between the following numbers: 1→2→3→5→6→7; 4→6.

The black arrows should be between 1→2 & 2→3.

And a blue arrow between 6→7.

All others should be red.

COLOURING NOTES 8.4

(a) The cingulate gyrus
(b) The amygdala
(c) The prefrontal cortex
(d) The hypothalamus

COLOURING NOTES 8.5

(a) Anger
(b) Fear
(c) Surprise
(d) Sadness
(e) Happiness
(f) Disgust

COLOURING NOTES 8.6

(a) The hypothalamus
(b) CRF
(c) The pituitary gland
(d) ACTH
(e) The adrenal cortex
(f) Cortisol

The feedback loop you have drawn should go from cortisol (f) to the hypothalamus (a) and pituitary gland (c).

CHAPTER 9

COLOURING NOTES 9.1

(a) Oesophagus
(b) Liver
(c) Duodenum
(d) Large intestine
(e) Small intestine
(f) Stomach

COLOURING NOTES 9.2

(a) The ARC
(b) The LH
(c) The PVN

The neurons that express NPY, AgRP, α MSH and POMC should be located in the ARC.

AgRP should have a blue line from the ARC (a) to the PVN (c).

NPY should have a red arrow from the ARC (a) to the PVN (c).

α MSH should have a red arrow from the ARC (a) to the LH (b).

LH should have a red arrow as it is involved in the promotion of eating.

PVN should have a blue arrow as it is involved in the inhibition of eating.

COLOURING NOTES 9.3

(a) Control (normal)
(b) Sweet
(c) Sour
(d) Bitter

COLOURING NOTES 9.4

(a) Mesocortical projections
(b) The amygdala
(c) Mesolimbic projections
(d) The VTA
(e) The nucleus accumbens

COLOURING NOTES 9.5

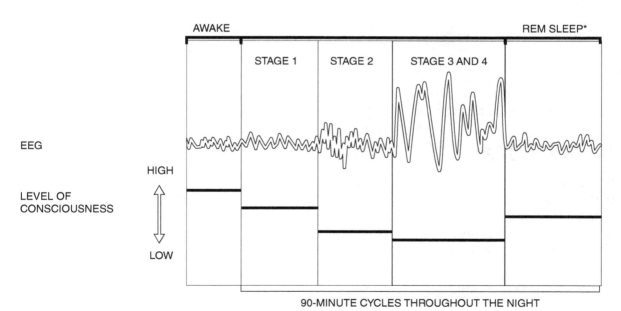

* REM sleep is similar to waking

Adapted from Bryant, P.A., et al. (2004). 'Sick and tired: does sleep have a vital role in the immune system?', *Nature Reviews Immunology*. With permission from the Copyright Clearance Centre: Springer Nature.

COLOURING NOTES 9.6

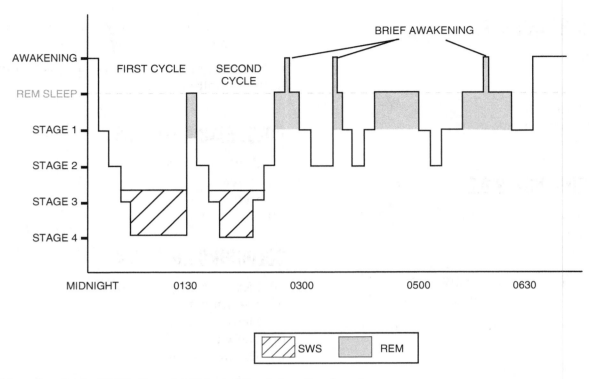

Adapted from Barnes, J., (2013). *Essential Biological Psychology*. London: Sage.

COLOURING NOTES 9.7

(a) Cortex
(b) Thalamus
(c) The basal forebrain
(d) Lateral hypothalamus
(e) The PPT/LDT
(f) The monoaminergic brainstem

Brainstem-thalamus-cortex pathway (in blue) should run from (e) to (b) and then (b) to (a).

Monoamine-lateral hypothalamus/basal forebrain-cortex pathway (in orange) should be the arrows between (f) to (d) and then (d) to (c).

COLOURING NOTES 9.8

(a) The cortex
(b) The thalamus
(c) The basal forebrain
(d) The lateral hypothalamus
(e) The ventrolateral preoptic nucleus
(f) PPT/LDT
(g) The monoaminergic brainstem

The inhibitory projections from the VLPO that inhibit arousal systems (in orange) runs from (e) to (g).

COLOURING NOTES 9.9

(A)

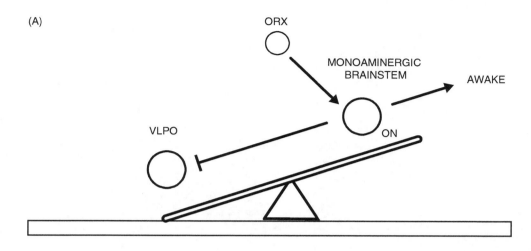

(B)

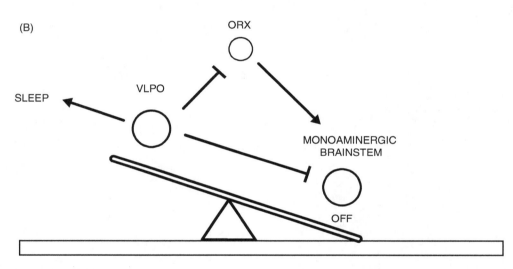

Adapted with permission of Wiley. From Saper et al. (2005). 'Homeostatic, circadian, and emotional regulation of sleep', *Journal of Comparative Neurology*, 493(1). Permission conveyed through Copyright Clearance Center, Inc.

The inhibitory projections should be drawn between the VLPO and the monoaminergic brainstem in (a). The activating projections should be between ORX and the monoaminergic brainstem in both (a) and (b).

CPSIA information can be obtained
at www.ICGtesting.com
Printed in the USA
BVHW010459230521
607766BV00006B/56